P9-DCX-359

Televising "Your Message

Producing Effective Television Communication

Wanda B. Mitchell

Former Supervisor, Speech Arts Department
Evanston Township High School, Illinois

James D. Kirkham

Coordinator of Instructional Television
High School District 205, Illinois

Instructor of Television Production
Thornton Community College, Illinois

NATIONAL TEXTBOOK COMPANY • *Skokie, IL 60077 U.S.A.*

Acknowledgments

viii *Dunagin's People* by Ralph Dunagin © 1972 Field Enterprises, Inc. Courtesy of Field Newspaper Syndicate.

5 *Animal Crackers* reprinted by permission of the Chicago Tribune-New York News Syndicate, Inc.

8 Magnovox Consumer Electronics

14, 16 Reprinted from Scholastic Magazine, by permission Ms. Louise Dates

12, 13, 207 CBS News Photos

18, 73 ABC Photos © 1980

25, 28, 29, 72 NBC Photo Services

32 WLS TV Photo

35 "Put Them All Together They Spell Television," by Robert Lasson and David Eynon, September 24, 1972. "© 1972 by The New York Times Company. Reprinted by permission."

43, 44 Bruce I. Bollatyne

45 Ampex Educational and Industrial Products Division, Elk Grove Village, IL 60007

85 Shure Brothers, Inc., Evanston, IL 60201

90 Electro-Voice, Inc., Buchanan, MI 49107

133 "Ten Commandments of Television" from THE TELEVISION PROGRAM: ITS DIRECTION AND PRODUCTION, Fifth Edition, by Edward Stasheff, Rudy Bretz, John Gartley, and Lynn Gartley. Copyright © 1976 by Ferrar, Straus, and Giroux, Inc. Reprinted by permission of Hill and Wang (a division of Ferrar, Straus, and Giroux, Inc.)

139 From STRICTLY PERSONAL by Sydney J. Harris. Copyright Field Enterprises, Inc. Courtesy of Field Newspaper Syndicate.

167 From Rod Serling's TWILIGHT ZONE REVISITED, adapted by Walter B. Gibson, Copyright © 1964 by Cayuga Productions, Inc. Used by permission of Grosset & Dunlap, Inc.

188, 190 Sony Corp. of America, Long Island City, N.Y. 11101

198 Photo from Educational and Industrial Television, by permission Howard Mark and Control Data Corp.

207 National Association of Educational Broadcasters for permission to reprint portions of NAEB Newsletter

190 RCA Photo

216 Photo of Carolyn Bailey and Patricia Phelps, courtesy WWMU-TV, West Virginia University

Thanks to Jeremiah Madden, director of television center; George Geyer; Norman Isacson; and television production students, Evanston Township (Illinois) High School for photos in TV studios. Also to Dr. Donald Kirkorian, television coordinator of Solano County Community College, Suisun City, Calif., and students of Fremont Union High School, Sunnyvale, Calif.

Dave Montgomery, Audio Visual Director, Thornton Twp. High School for many of the photos used in the book; John Malloy, Radio TV instructor, Thornton Twp. High School; Eric Szambaris, student at Thornton Twp. High School, for allowing me to use his script for a class assignment; to all the students in Radio TV Production classes at Thornton Twp. High School for making teaching fun.

The following companies supplied information on products described in this book: Bell & Howell, Chicago, Ill.; Center for Cassette Studies, Inc., North Hollywood, Calif.; Electronic Specialty Co., Charlestown, W. Va. 25302; Panasonic CCTV-VTR, New York, N.Y.; Singer Co., Binghampton, N.Y.; Telemation, Inc., Salt Lake City, Utah; and Teleprompter, New York, N.Y.

Visual Studies Workshop
Research Center
Rochester, N.Y.

Copyright © 1981 by National Textbook Co.,
8259 Niles Center Rd., Skokie, Ill. 60077
Library of Congress Catalog Number: 80-80891
All rights reserved. No part of this book
may be reproduced, stored in a retrieval system, or
transmitted in any form or by any means, electronic,
mechanical, photocopying, recording or otherwise,
without the prior permission of National Textbook Company.
Manufactured in the United States of America.

0 PP 9 8 7 6 5 4 3 2 1

Contents

Introduction

In ancient times, when Rome, not electronic media, ruled the world, a great communicator, Seneca by name, proclaimed, "If a ship does not know to which port it is sailing, no wind is good." This need for clearly stated goals is equally applicable to a textbook, especially if that book treats an area as all-inclusive as television.

Televising Your Message is concerned with the human, persuasive, and communicative elements in the process of transmitting a message from the sender to the receiver through the medium of television. It aims to inform the sender how to use television effectively to get a message across to the viewer; it is not simply a communication or media handbook.

While this book imparts valuable information about the tools, techniques, and terminology needed to produce effective and efficient communication in the television studio, it is not a technical lab manual. *Televising Your Message* provides simplified experiences for students who want to learn what is involved in preparing and presenting a television program in a classroom, on a closed circuit cable, or on a public or commercial station.

Because of its broad scope and basic approach, *Televising Your Message* need not be confined to television production classes. It can be used effectively as a unit in mass communications, language arts, journalism, and social studies classes as well.

Televising Your Message promotes high standards for the writing, producing, and directing of any television presentation, whether it be for the classroom or a major television network. At the same time, this text explains the psychological, artistic, and communication principles as they apply to any type of telecast, and attempts to develop evaluative criteria by which the viewer can critically analyze programs.

Within each chapter of this text, students are afforded the opportunity to evaluate, discuss, and extend the material presented in the "Take Two" section. The "Videolab" sections, also found at the end of each chapter, offer students creative laboratory activities designed to provide experience in production techniques and stimulate effective television communication. The "Testing 1-2-3" section in the appendix gives students a chance to review and test their knowledge.

Finally, this book tries to light a spark of interest in the student that, tempered with high hope and healthy skepticism, will motivate him or her to explore on his or her own the rapidly changing professional opportunities in the medium, as well as its technology and humanity.

Televising Your Message is offered to those who believe that the most skillful and most responsible use of this medium of communication is essential to guarantee free speech in America.

W. B. Mitchell
J. D. Kirkham

"THIS STUFF IS PRETTY ADULT. ISN'T THERE ANYTHING ON WITH SOME VIOLENCE IN IT?"

Viewing the Message

By the time one graduates from high school, the average young person has watched more than 15,000 hours of television, having spent only 10,800 hours in school. A recent edition of *Broadcasting*, a professional journal for broadcasters, notes that the average family spends six hours and thirty-four minutes viewing TV every day. Television is the most widely used form of recreation, as well as the only information source for many Americans. Add to this the hours that will be spent with home video recorders, videodiscs, and home computer terminals, and the importance of the television set to our daily lives is multiplied.

Why Do You Watch Television?

If you're a boy and are short on cash the night you have a date, you and your girlfriend can always stay home (hers or yours) and watch television. If you're a girl and you have to babysit and do your homework at the same time, you can always seat the children in front of the television set until they fall asleep. If the northern winds are howling and the temperature is hovering near zero, you can watch a movie on television rather than trudge through the snow to a movie theater. If you can't afford a weekend in South Bend, Indiana, you can watch Notre Dame play Southern California on television. If life is getting you down and everything's turning out wrong, you can tune in a variety show, mystery, or drama and forget your troubles for an hour.

Do you ever watch television because your favorite movie star or some famous sports figure is being featured on a special? Do you read a newspaper ad for a new program and tune in because it sounds interesting? Do you tune in a "special" because the previews aroused your curiosity? Just why do you watch television?

A survey of four hundred freshmen in a midwestern high school indicated that they watched television primarily for entertainment. For those freshmen, even the instructive programs of the Public Broadcasting Service ranked higher than the news, which was selected least often.

Television is an entertainer, a journalist, a teacher, and a salesperson. Your reasons for watching television will determine your attitude toward these four types of programs and will determine how you decode or interpret the messages they convey. Just as the intended function of a program determines its point of view, your reason for viewing it affects your perception of the program. If you expect to be entertained, you will be unhappy to receive a lecture on economics.

What Determines Which Specific Programs You Watch?

Until recently, what you watched was determined by what was shown by the television stations in your area. Many cities could only pick up one or two stations. With new technology, this has changed. Let's examine all the factors that determine what we watch.

Broadcast stations. Most of us still receive our TV programs from the major networks (CBS, NBC, ABC, PBS). Networks and advertisers spend millions of dollars on programs that will bring them viewers, and in turn, profits for the network or stations. American television is different from television in many parts of the world. Would you believe in some countries, there are no commercials at all? Viewers are taxed according to the number of TV sets in the house. Other countries control the television programming and use TV primarily for propaganda purposes. In the United States, we, too, pay for our TV programs, but we pay for them with our time. The networks, advertisers, and local stations want us to view the commercials as well as the programs. Advertisers are willing to spend as much as $300,000 for one minute of our time during the Super Bowl telecast. To advertisers, television is often the most economical way to reach millions of viewers at one time.

Most of the programs seen on TV are shown on the networks as the local stations have little opportunity to pay for programs all day long. A few independent stations (ones not affiliated with any network) purchase syndicated programs that have already appeared on the networks. Some larger independent stations, such as WTCG in Atlanta and WGN in Chicago, are not dependent on the networks. Yet most of the television stations only broadcast 11 percent of their own programs. The rest comes from networks or syndication.

Ratings. Perhaps the most important influence on what you watch is *you*. Since advertisers are trying to reach as many people as possible, they have created a system that measures the number of people viewing specific programs at one time. Ratings are a scientific, efficient method of telling how many people actually viewed a particular program. They are important to broadcasters and advertisers alike. Advertisers use them to determine if they are getting the most for their advertising dollar. Programs that do not "pull a good rating" mean that advertisers are not reaching the largest audience and should perhaps look elsewhere to place the ads.

Ratings are important to broadcasters because they know how many people are viewing the television program. If most people are viewing the program on one station, more money could be charged for airing the commercial during this program. For example, if the program is very successful in the ratings, the network might charge as much as $135,000 for a thirty-second "spot" (commercial), and there will probably be at least three opportunities for the airing of this spot during the program. Using a little mathematics, this could add up to $405,000 for commercial time during this particular show. If the program runs poorly in the ratings, the network may only charge $60,000 to run the same commercial; this means gross profit would only come to $180,000 for the network. There is a big difference, and now one can understand why ratings are important. Programs are often dropped if they do not create a profit. Some programs are seen only a few times before they are dropped in favor of a more popular one. Some programs such as *Meet the Press, Wonderful World of Disney,* and *The Tonight Show* seem to go on forever. This kind of longevity, however, is rare.

Since ratings are a very important part of the broadcast industry, it is a good idea to examine how they are determined. Ratings services, such as AC Nielson, ARB, Trendex, and Pusle, poll a very scientific sample of viewers to determine the number of viewers at a specific time. Now they have overnight services in the large cities such as New York, Chicago, and Los Angeles to get instant ratings on important programs. One of the largest ratings services uses computer terminals connected to the television sets of a carefully selected sample of about 1200 viewers. When their televisions are on, the channel is automatically monitored by a computer in Florida. The rating service can instantly determine what these viewers are watching. Using a very scientific study known as sampling, they can predict how these 1200 viewers will represent other viewers across the country. Other sampled viewers are given diaries to keep for one month. Even though the methods are often criticized by the radio and television industry and by those performers whose contracts are not renewed, the ratings have a strong influence on network schedules. During a ratings week, the competition for viewers may result in three top-flight programs being shown by the three networks at one time. During one ratings week, for example, viewers had to choose between the films, *One Flew Over the Cuckoos Nest, Gone with the Wind,* and a made for TV movie, *Elvis.*

FCC regulations. Another influence upon the programs available to you is the FCC, the Federal Communications Commission. Made up of seven commissioners appointed for seven-year terms by the President with the approval of the Senate, the FCC directs the development of the nation's broadcasting services. The commissioners allocate spectrum or wavelength space for police, shortwave, and CB broadcasts. They determine which frequency a radio station may use and which channel a television station may use. They decide, for instance, that WBMZ-TV will transmit on Channel 5, that station WMOA will broadcast at 710 on your AM radio, and that WMOA-FM will broadcast at 95.2 on your FM radio. Without such regulations and assignments, you would be able to hear and see nothing because the broadcasts would jam each other and chaos would result. However, there is talk of deregulating radio and television stations. Soon it may be possible that stations will be granted licenses for life and will not have to renew their commitment every three years.

The FCC grants broadcasting licenses to applicants who can meet technical broadcasting standards and agree to operate in the "public interest, convenience, and necessity." Furthermore, every three years the FCC reviews each station's performance to determine whether or not it has met the requirements of its license. These last two functions of the Commission directly affect what the stations show or do not show on television. If a station's percentage of public service programs is running low when license-renewal time approaches, college debates and high school music programs are suddenly given unaccustomed priority—as evidence that the station is operating in the public interest.

FCC regulations exercise another kind of control over the availability of programs you can watch. To ensure fairness, a station that gives or sells time for one side of a controversial issue must grant an equal opportunity to the opposite point of view. This is called the *Fairness Doctrine*.

The equal time provision requires a broadcast station to give absolute equal time to all qualified candidates for an election. For instance, during the 1972 presidential campaign, the *Dinah Shore Show* had to wait until after the November election to present a previously taped show featuring vice-presidential candidate Sargent Shriver with his wife and three children. Although Dinah Shore had done a show with Vice-President Agnew in 1971, she wasn't permitted to do one with a vice-presidential candidate in an election year. Eliminated from the same series were a baby picture of presidential candidate George McGovern and a picture of President Richard Nixon dancing with daughter Tricia at her wedding. In the 1976 and 1980 elections, many TV stations refused to show Ronald Reagan's older movies. They feared if these were shown, other candidates might have demanded equal time.

Cable TV.   Cable television is not new. Actually, cable was developed in the 1950s in order to bring television reception to areas that were too far from broadcast stations or were blocked by terrain. In recent years, cable TV has grown, and it is estimated there are now over 3000 cable systems in homes. It is estimated that by 2000, over 90 percent of the homes will be receiving TV by a cable system. A cable company will erect large antennas and satellite receivers and wire the homes to receive as many as thirty-six channels of programs.

In addition to the networks, many independent stations can be received by viewers. Some stations, such as WTCG in Atlanta and WGN in Chicago, are being carried by satellite to independent cable companies and are seen in forty-six states. Cable companies can also provide the latest uncut movies, which will not be shown on network television. It is now possible to view the latest movie without having to go to the theater. The U.S. Congress offers coverage of Congressional proceedings for cable subscribers. Many local cable companies also telecast high school and college sports events, as well as town and school board meetings. They can offer programs such as these because they do not have to rely on ratings or advertisers for their revenue. They simply charge a monthly fee for the service.

It is also possible to provide police and fire alarm protection through the cable TV hookup. Some of the newer systems also offer two-way communication so viewers can respond to questions offered at town meetings. It might be said that it's a way to talk back to the TV set!

Home video recorders.   Until recently, only television stations, schools, or large businesses could afford the large video tape recorders. Often costing as much as $150,000, most homes could not even consider owning one. However, with new technology this has changed, and it is now possible that most homes will have video recording equipment in the near future. It is estimated that over 100,000 video recorders are sold every month. Viewers

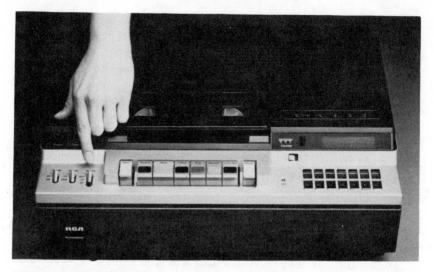

Home recorders are allowing families to produce their own TV programs and shift their TV viewing time.

The new 2-inch videotape cassette recorder can program short commercials back-to-back with no threading.

can now view two programs at once by recording one channel while viewing another. If your favorite movie comes on at 1 AM, you can set the recorder to record the movie and view it at your convenience. This, however, has presented some problems to broadcasters. It may not be possible to know how many viewers are watching or recording programs, so it will be hard to determine how much to charge advertisers.

Recently, the legality of recording programs under current copyright laws has been determined. Many movie producers didn't want viewers to record their programs off the air as this could limit attendance in theaters. A recent court case in California, however, ruled individuals could record TV programs off the air and view them later. With these new recorders, it is possible to purchase or rent the latest movies. Some of the more popular movies can be rented for home recorders soon after they are shown in theaters. Some libraries check out movies. These newer home recorders can also record home movies on video tape. This means that many families are becoming TV producers, too.

Video Discs.   In addition to home recorders, it is now possible to purchase a record player that not only allows you to hear your favorite musical group in stereo, but also will allow you to *see* them in color on your television set. It may soon be possible to buy your favorite movie in the supermarket as you check out. Plans have begun to put the *Sears Catalog* on video disc so you can shop at home on your TV set. Currently, there is competition between two major companies and, there is no compatability between machines. With the newer technology, we no longer have to depend on the three major television networks for our entertainment or information.

History of Broadcasting

Much of what we watch on television developed from early radio. Believe it or not, television is still a relatively young medium. Newspapers, for example, have been in the United States since about 1700. The telegraph was invented in 1844. The telephone was developed in 1876, and the first commercially licensed radio station went on the air in 1920. KDKA in Pittsburg, Pennsylvania began broadcasting on November 2, 1920 with the Cox-Harding election results and still broadcasts today.

Television, on the other hand, really didn't begin to come into homes until 1948. Before television, people listened to the radio. In fact, many of our favorite TV programs developed from earlier radio broadcasts. During the day, housewives listened to their favorite soap operas on radio. Instead of watching *As the World Turns*, *General Hospital*, and *Guiding Light*, they listened to *Old Ma Perkins* and *Romance of Helen Trent*.

In the evening, the family turned to adventure programs or to variety and situation comedies. *The Lone Ranger* was one of the longest running radio programs. Other great programs included *Suspense*, *Inner Sanctum*, and *Gangbusters*. Long before *I Love Lucy* came to television, families were laughing about the problems of *Blondie*, *Henry Aldrich*, and *The Nelson Family* on the radio. Many of the recent situation comedies such as *Mork and Mindy* and *Happy Days* developed their ideas from earlier radio programs.

Because broadcasting history is important to anyone seriously interested in the field of mass communications and broadcasting, here is a capsule history of broadcasting.

Broadcasting History

1915:   University of Wisconsin begins experimental radio station.

1916:   Pittsburgh begins second experimental radio station.

1920:   KDKA-Pittsburgh begins 1st regular broadcasting on November 2.

1920:   WWJ-Detroit claims *it* was 1st on August 20.

1921:   WBZ-Springfield, Mass. issued 1st regular broadcasting license by U.S. Dept. of Commerce.

1922:   WEAF-New York broadcasts 1st sponsored program. Advertising begins.

1923:   National Association of Broad-Casters (NAB) formed.

1923:   WEAF-New York & WNAC-Boston complete 1st network hook up (a football game).

1925:   1st "chain broadcasting". 24 stations across continent carry Coolidge inauguration.

1926:   RCA buys ATT&T's radio properties & forms National Broadcasting Company with 24 stations. David Sarnoff is 1st president of NBC.

1927:   NBC broadcasts New Year's day Rose Bowl game over 19 stations.

1927:   United Independent Broadcasters (UIB), later Columbia Broadcasting System (CBS), begins with 16 stations. LaPalina Cigar heir, William S. Paley, buys the network.

1927: Federal Radio Commission (FRC) established to issue station-only licenses, allocate frequencies & bands. Acts against air "pirates"

1931: CBS begins, on an experimental basis, 1st regularly scheduled TV with New York Mayor Jimmy Walker & singer Kate Smith.

1932: "Amos & Andy" goes on air from Chicago on NBC.

1933: President Franklin D. Roosevelt uses all radio networks for 4 "fireside chats" to talk directly to the American people.

1934: Mutual Broadcasting System (MBS) established.

1934: Federal Communications Commission (FCC) established to issue *all* radio licenses & renewals, allocate frequencies, & decide on AM, FM, & Educational FM.

1934: CBS *School of the Air* is 1st commercial network education show.

1936: 1st network raid. CBS lures Major Bowles Amateur Hour from NBC.

1938: Radio's Golden Age of Radio begins. Networks expand. Variety, drama, & action programs flourish. Golden Ages lasts until 1948 when TV begins to take over variety, drama & adventure programming.

1941: World War II begins. Broadcasting brings the war into the home. CBS broadcasts 35,700 war programs. By end of war there are 56,000,000 radio sets & 16,500 TV sets.

1945: FM Radio established. Both FM & TV broadcasting held up by WW II.

1945: Dr. Peter Golmark of CBS develops long playing (LP), 33 rpm record & color television.

1948: Ed Sullivan Show, Milton Berle Show, Arthur Godfrey Show begin on TV.

1948: Radio changes drastically in order to compete with TV's popularity.

1952: Golden Age of TV begins with shows like *Playhouse 90*, *Studio One*.

1953: CBS-TV becomes world's largest single advertising medium. Stays that way for 10 years straight.

1955: New adult western, *Gunsmoke*, switches from radio to TV and inspires host of imitators.

1955: Edward R. Murrow does expose on *I See it Now* about Wisconsin Senator Joseph McCarthy. Spells end of McCarthyism & Blacklisting.

1955: 1st TV quiz show debuts. *$64,000 Question*.

1958: 1st stereo record marketed by CBS. Spurs beginning of Stereo-FM radio.

1959: Broadcasting hit with "payola" & TV quiz show scandals.

1959: James Aubrey, new CBS-TV president, set tone for TV programming by featuring innocuous, mindless programming. Gives rise to "vast wasteland" charge.

1963: President John F. Kennedy shot in Dallas, Texas. Networks abandon all commercial broadcasting for 4 straight days & nights.

1968: TV news is criticized for too much coverage on city & campus riots and anti-war protests. Violence of 1968 Democratic Nat'l Convention broadcast to the world.

1969: The world watches over 24 hours continual coverage of man's first steps on the moon's surface.

How Do You Watch Television?

Television is not only watched for entertainment, but also for information. What do *you* watch? Now comes the payoff. How do you watch? Do you absorb like a sponge? Are you critically selective? Are you a spectator or a participant? Can you tell from the commercials what kind of viewer the advertiser thinks you are—perceptive, gullible, conservative, liberal, critical, adventurous, romantic, creative, unimaginative, young, old, sophisticated, homespun, square?

When you watch the news, do you consider all the newscasters fair and unbiased? In his book *The Newscasters*, critic Ron Powers charges that the newscasts at 10 PM are often misleading in order to attract viewers for higher ratings. He claims that often uninteresting or nonvisual stories are dropped in order to make room for emotional or stimulating stories designed to catch your attention. "Soft news" features such as

Despite the fact that television, as all news media, has been accused of biased reporting, TV coverage is still thought to be the fairest of all.

Dan Rather, CBS correspondent and Co-editor of *60 Minutes* will replace Walter Cronkite as anchorman for the CBS Evening News.

reports on soap operas, nutrition, or film reviews are added because viewers seem to express interest in these. Newscasts now are big money-makers to stations and often become vaudeville shows to attract viewers.

Recently, the Opinion Research Corporation of Princeton, N.J., conducted a poll for *TV Guide* to determine Americans' opinions of political coverage and its fairness. When people were asked, "Which of the four major news media (magazines, newspapers, radio, and television) do you think is fairest and most objective in its political reporting and coverage?" Fifty-three percent preferred television; fifteen percent, newspapers; eight percent, magazines; seven percent, radio; and seventeen percent had no opinion. "Which network do you think is fairest and most objective in its political reporting and coverage, or do you think there is no difference among the networks in this respect?" One out of every two persons either saw no difference among the networks (forty percent) or had no opinion (eleven percent).

Some viewers prefer television to radio because they like to look into the speakers' eyes, to judge for themselves how reliable they are by the way they look and act, not just by what they say. Do you agree with those who contend that nonverbal clues, observable in tight close-ups of a speaker's face, make it virtually impossible for a political candidate to hide his or her true feelings in a speech of thirty minutes or more?

Scholastic magazine offered this rating chart as a guide for more critical listening and viewing.

Radio-TV News Rating Chart

EASY TO UNDERSTAND (Is the news given in the simplest, clearest way possible?)

_____ Are the most important news events of the day covered first?

_____ Are the sentences short and easy to understand?

_____ Does the newscaster carefully pronounce difficult words and names of foreign places and people?

_____ Are the unfamiliar names of people and places identified? (Example: Teheran, the capital of Iran)

_____ Does the newscaster give you some background information to help you understand the day's news?

RELIABILITY (Does the newscaster make it clear whether he's giving a fact or an opinion?)

_____ When he gives an opinion or interpretation, does he tell his listeners whose opinion or interpretation he's giving?

_____ Does he control his voice so as to avoid giving hints of his personal opinion?

_____ Is he careful to give enough of the facts of the story so that you can arrive at a sound personal opinion based on the facts?

FAIR-MINDEDNESS (When there are two or more sides to a question, does the newscaster present all sides fairly?)

_____ Does he avoid "pet peeves" (dislike of a particular party, etc.)?

_____ Does he avoid promoting pet projects or ideas?

_____ Does he avoid showing his personal likes and dislikes for certain people?

_____ Does he try to show people and events as they are—a mixture of good and bad?

_____ Does he explain news in the light of the facts (give facts to support his opinions)?

_____ Does he try to present all viewpoints on a particular question? (For example: Does he tell how both the Democrats and Republicans view a particular situation?)

_____ Does he interpret various viewpoints with equal weight?

ORGANIZATION (Does he make the most of the time at his disposal?)

_____ Does he give adequate time and emphasis to the big news stories of the day?

_____ Does he make the most of his time by carefully avoiding talk that is merely "cute"?

QUALIFICATIONS (Is the newscaster well qualified for his job?)

_____ Has he had a thorough education for his job? (Long experience may be considered educational.)

_____ Has he had experience in gathering news?

_____ Has he received a top award for his work as a newsman?[1]

Can you observe any clues, both verbal and nonverbal, to the newscaster's personal opinion about the news he or she is presenting? Do you ever discuss with other students, in or out of class, the news and the way it is presented? Do you like the same newscasters as your parents? As your older brother or sister? Why or why not?

Background. How you watch television and how critically you react depend upon your personal background, interests, prejudices, and knowledge. If your background includes several years of living in New York City before you moved to Keokuk, Iowa, you will watch a television play about a fire in a New York subway more critically than your Keokuk friends will. Since they do not know as you do what it means to travel twice a day on the subway, they cannot judge how true to life the story is.

If you have always attended symphony concerts and have studied the violin since you were seven, you watch the struggles of a young musical artist sacrificing for his or her art more sympathetically than the viewer who has never tried to create music.

If your father and two older brothers have been varsity football players in high school and college, you watch the pro football games on television with the understanding you have absorbed merely by listening to their dinner conversation.

The doctor sees a different medical show; the teacher sees a different education documentary; the police officer a different crime drama. Because of their personal experiences, viewers differ in their appraisal of those programs and even television personalities with which they are most familiar.

The comedian on a variety show may not get through to you because his or her vocabulary and "in" jokes are from another era, which your parents know about and therefore enjoy. It is frequently hard to believe there are actually families like those as portrayed on television. Yet many people view these programs because they can identify with many of the characters or problems in the television families.

Gags based on ethnic or religious idioms may get no laugh from you, while other viewers who are familiar with these cultures find them hilariously funny. Can you tell when the humor lags because of what you, the viewer, bring or do not bring to the program?

How you watch and react is determined to a considerable degree by how you are in the habit of reacting to all elements of your environment. According to legend, John Burroughs, the naturalist, and a banker friend were strolling together along a noisy side street near Times Square, New York. Suddenly Burroughs halted and grabbed his companion by the arm. "Listen! Hear that cricket?" The banker ridiculed the idea that anyone could hear the chirp of a cricket in all that traffic din. What would it be doing there anyway? Burroughs, however, insisted he had heard a cricket and proved he was right when he spotted it among the fruits and vegetables on a peddler's pushcart at the curb. A few blocks farther up the street, the banker grabbed Burrough's arm and halted him with the exclamation, "Someone dropped a coin. I heard a quarter hit the pavement." This time, it was Burroughs' turn to scoff at the audio acuity of his friend until the banker pointed to a coin on the metal sewer grill at the curb. The story may be fictional, but the lesson is obvious. One sees and hears what one is trained to see and hear.

Suppose you habitually look at everything from a conservative point of view. What kind of person will you see in Archie Bunker? If certain programs affect you differently than they do some of your friends, can you tell why? Take, for example, your grandmother, who has been trained to listen to the melody in music and prefers Lawrence Welk or Liberace rather than Fleetwood Mac or the Rolling Stones, whose rhythms provide the kind of music you are trained to enjoy.

How do you watch? Do you select only the programs you know and like? If a show doesn't appeal to you, does the reason lie in you or in the program? When you watch a dramatic show, can you separate the shoddy from the artistic? Can you analyze what you see and hear well enough to answer these questions from a rating chart in *Scholastic* magazine?

Rating Chart for Radio-Television Dramatic Shows

THEME (What the drama is about)
1. Was the story important to your life rather than about characters who are farfetched or phony?
2. Was the action of the show that of two forces of people or ideas, one wanting something and the other fighting to keep it from him, rather than senseless activity?
3. Did it help you to understand yourself and other people better?

STORY (Plot)
1. Did the writing give the story oral (radio) and visual (television)

rhythm by presenting characters in motion, not merely in mental conflict?

2. Could you imagine yourself experiencing what one of the characters was experiencing?
3. Did the story develop naturally to a definite climax and a logical ending?
4. Were all the incidents, local color, etc., essential to the story, and was every detail that was nonessential (even though "cute") left out?
5. Was the story well written (or adapted) for radio or television?

PRODUCTION AND DIRECTION
1. Was the total effect of the production unusually artistic, realistic, or powerful?
2. Were the actors well chosen for their roles?
3. Did the action of the show flow along smoothly and understandably?

CHARACTERIZATION (Acting and speech)
1. Did the actors speak clearly, varying the tempo and pitch of their voices according to what they were saying?
2. Did the actors make the characters "come alive"?
3. Did the actors seem to know exactly what they were supposed to be doing at every given moment?
4. Did the actors stir you emotionally, make you cry or laugh or think?

SOUND AND MUSICAL EFFECTS
1. Were the sound effects well timed and effective?
2. Did the music set the correct mood for the show?
3. Was it the right music for the style of the show (such as clavichord music for an 18th century English play)?
4. Did the music flow smoothly from one theme to another?
5. Did the music help you to feel the passing of time?
6. Was the music well played?

FOR RADIO DRAMATIC SHOWS ONLY
1. Did the dialogue help you to "see" (in your mind's eye) the scene and action of the characters?
2. Did the actors have contrasting voices, making it easy for you to know which one was talking?
3. Did the music prepare you, the listener, for what was going to happen next?
4. Did the music help you to "see" the scene?

What Effect Does Television Viewing Have on You?

How do you let it affect you? Can you avoid its influence? Should you avoid its influence?

Television has the ability to give each viewer a box seat at the World Series. As a result, fan expectations create new pressures on athletes.

Television certainly has affected the amount of information readily available to you. Mature programs and adult experiences are yours at the flick of a switch. Even the youngest member of your family acquires information formerly reserved for adults. Kindergarten teachers report that "detergent" is now in the vocabulary of the preschool child, who can also, thanks to television commercials, select cereals and packaged foods from the shelves of the supermarket before he or she has learned to read. Educational programs such as *Sesame Street* have taught children how to read and count long before entering kindergarten.

Think of the misconceptions that have been avoided because television brings people with lifestyles that are totally different into your life. The child of the ghetto of a big city can see what it's like to live on a farm; the suburban student can witness conditions in a city barrio; the merchant in Oshkosh, Wisconsin, can see what life is like in Hong Kong; the ranch hand in Montana can watch a nightclub act in Las Vegas. You, as a critical viewer, can heighten your sensitivity if you study what you see and use your information for making judgments.

Education increases your power to suffer in the same way that it develops your ability to enjoy. For instance, the more you know about baseball, the more you can enjoy the skillful maneuvering of the pitcher and base stealer—but at the same time the more you suffer when you see stupid blunders and unforgivable errors. The more you learn about music, the more you can appreciate the rich timbre of a lovely voice with perfect attack and true pitch. The tone-deaf listener who knows nothing about music does not cringe at the "sour" note, which is agonizing for the true musician.

Thus it is with your knowledge of television. The more you learn about it—why you watch what you watch, the different points of view as determined by the different functions—the more you become aware of how to watch and of how you are affected by what you watch. In other words, the more "TV-educated" you become, the more you will enjoy and appreciate programs that are well done, and the more you will suffer during shoddy, trite, and ill-conceived programs.

Take Two

1. Why do you think the government regulates radio and television stations but does not regulate newspapers?

2. Broadcasters must promise to broadcast in the public "interest, need, and convenience." Do you think most broad-

casters are providing programs to meet these requirements? Why or why not?

3. Why are ratings so important to radio and television stations? How do the ratings affect programming?

4. If you were a TV producer or network president, how would you feel about video recorders and video discs? How do you think they will affect TV in the future?

5. In your opinion, how important is the visual appeal (film or tape) to television news?

6. How does radio differ today from the programs heard before there was television? Why do you think radio changed after television?

7. Why is the local newscast so important to a TV station?

8. *Broadcasting* magazine stated the average family spends six hours and thirty-four minutes viewing television every day. Keep a daily record of viewing in your family for several days. How does your family compare with the average?

> *Categories*
> Situation comedies
> Family shows
> Medical, detective, police stories
> Sports
> Game shows
> News and public affairs programs
> Talk, variety, interview shows
> Soap operas
> Specials
> Children's shows
> Individual dramas and miniseries
> Public Broadcasting Service programs
> Music, concert programs
> Religious programs
> Nature shows

1. If a baseball fan never sees a track meet, it is difficult and somewhat uninteresting for him or her to compare the speed of a batter covering bases with the speed of a 100-yard-dash runner. If all you ever watch on television is situation comedy, you are missing a broad expanse of enjoyable programs. During a six-week period, try to watch two or three programs in each of the following categories. (It isn't fair to pass judgment after seeing only one program in a series; any show may have an off night.)

Select one of the programs you have watched in each of the categories. Identify the program, and write a critique of the show using the following questions:

   a. For whom is the program intended? Can you tell for whom it is intended by the hour at which it is shown or by the type of commercials or sponsors?

   b. What is the point of view of the program? For instance, does a medical character exhibit a point of view toward socialized medicine, toward general practitioners, toward mental illness?

   c. Does it portray life realistically?

   d. Does it entertain, or inform, or instruct, or sell? Or do all these? For instance, why would the National Safety Council request that Robert Young, former star of the highly successful *Marcus Welby* series, be seen wearing a shoulder belt whenever he was in his car?

   e. What is the message of this program?

   f. What kind of person would get the most out of this program? To whom would you recommend it?

   g. Would you watch it again?

   h. What effect, if any, did it have on your actions and/or your opinions?

2. Create a two-minute radio program called "Someone You Should Know" to be used as a feature on a radio station. In this program, highlight the life or career of someone influential in the field of broadcasting. Famous people such as David Sarnoff, Edward R. Morrow, Fred Friendly, Walter Cronkite, or many others could be featured in your

two-minute program. Tape record the program after researching and writing the script.

3. Keep a log for a thirty-minute television newscast. List each story used and note if the story had accompanying film or video tape. Which reports were more interesting? Did the order follow from the most to least important?

4. Keep another log for a local newscast for one week. Determine which stories were used to hold your attention. How many stories were "soft news" (special reports, consumer affairs, tabloid stories, and other non-news items)?

5. Watch the *MacNeil/Lehrer Report* on PBS and compare its format with the news on ABC, CBS, or NBC.

6. Keep a log of twenty-five commercials seen on television for one week. Note the product; how was it visualized? What emotional appeal was used to sell the product (security, physical attractiveness, love for family)?

7. Bring in ten ads from newspapers or magazines and identify the many different emotional appeals used to sell these products.

8. Become familiar with trade journals by reading a copy of *Broadcasting*. Write a two-page report on what you found inside. Why are so many radio and television jobs listed?

9. Pretend you are a radio/TV critic for a local newspaper. Using the criteria found in this chapter, write a review for a network program such as *Little House on the Prairie*.

10. Keep a diary for two full weeks listing everything you watched on TV. Include the time, the program, the date, the channel, and number of viewers in your home. Compare your diary with those of your classmates. Then set up a class ratings system to determine if your viewing habits are different from the others.

11. Viewers are always complaining about the number of commercials interrupting movies. Watch an entire movie (with a stopwatch), keeping track of the total amount of time devoted to commercials. Does it exceed the amount permitted by the code requirements of the National Association of Broadcasters? (See page 160.)

2

Assessing the Medium

"Go, Wildkits!" cheer two dirty tennis shoes as they alternately hit the pavement with a verb and a noun lettered on their sides.

"This lemon was purchased from McWhorter Motors, 16 West Broad Street" is the message in ten-inch high, iridescent letters on the side of a new station wagon in the shopping center parking lot.

A teenager and a disgruntled car owner each selected what he and she considered the most appropriate medium for an idea to communicate to anyone who would look his and her way. But it is not always easy to decide the best way to get a message across. Advertisers have a variety of media from which to choose to reach the public. Radio, television, magazines, newspapers, and billboards are a few ways they can publicize their products.

In most schools, students also have a variety of media from which to choose. If your message is "Come to the school play," you may tell your story on posters, on the public address system, in the school newspaper, on the school radio, in skits in classrooms or on the auditorium stage, in conversation in the cafeteria, or in visual exhibits in a display case. Before making a choice, you listen to student reactions and comments "Nobody ever listens to the P.A. bulletin." "We don't have time to do a skit." "Everyone will see that kind of poster—why don't we make three?" "That idea's just plain stupid." You consider all these comments from fellow students and then select the most effective means, instrument, or medium for getting students to attend the play. You learn quickly which medium (newspaper, radio, television, posters, theater) is the most powerful in your school.

If you are campaigning for an office on the student council, how do you select the medium through which you will sell yourself to the student voters? How should seniors decide which of their activities will be reported in the school paper, which will be memorialized in the yearbook, which will be pressed onto an LP record, which will be recorded on film in the senior movie, and which recorded on a video cassette? Which messages are most effective in print? Supermarkets evidently prefer to publish their price lists and coupon sales in the newspaper for consumers to reread and use in making shopping lists. Which messages leave a more lasting impression when the words have the additional impact provided by the human voice? Does a live theatrical performance, with its emotional power, communicate more effectively than a record or a tape? Does television have a characteristic impact of its own, or is it merely a combination of the pictures and sounds of other media? How does theater differ from television? Can television do anything theater cannot do?

Two Kinds of Audience

To compare television and the stage as media for communicating ideas, you must first consider the two audiences, because to sell an idea you must know the potential buyer. In the theater, the audience is seated and usually remains seated for the entire performance, having come there to see a two-hour presentation. A member of the audience who becomes bored and walks out during the performance disturbs surrounding people and may even distract the performers on the stage. The television audience, on the other hand, comes and goes at will, switching from channel to channel at any point during the program with no immediate effect on the performers. Viewers may tune in after the program is well underway; two characters may have already died, or the opposing point of view may have already been presented.

Comedians performing on stage depend upon the response of the audience, their laughter and applause. They soon learn that the Wednesday matinee crowd of shoppers will not react to the same gags that delight the Saturday night celebrators. A television comedian often demands a studio audience, believing that the sound of laughter affects the home viewing audience. Recorded laugh tracks have been tried for situation comedies, but most viewers can recognize "canned" laughter, and many directors have dispensed with it in favor of a studio audience. Some acts are changed slightly for the benefit of this studio audience. Taped shows with studio audiences can be identified by the statement, "Recorded before a live audience."

NBC's successful *Saturday Night Live* has provided national exposure for bright young comedians.

Television and stage audiences differ in another respect: the circumstances that accompany their viewing situation. Students watching *Hamlet* on a classroom television set with a supervising teacher keep their eyes open and their faces turned toward the screen, regardless of where their thoughts are. Those same students, watching *Hamlet* on portable sets at the foot of their beds, may doze off now and then during "talky" scenes. If they take a special date to see *Hamlet* at the college theater, as part of a delightful evening "on the town," their concentration may not be on the staged production.

A young person watching a football game alone may remain quietly seated before the television set, except for occasional trips to the refrigerator. Two other people watching the same game may shout at each other and wave their arms, dodging the tacklers on television. A crowd watching the same game in Kansas City's Truman Sports Complex may cheer as wildly at the instant replay on the stadium's huge television screen as they do during the actual play on the field.

Another difference between the television and stage audience lies in the degree of control of the viewer's attention. The theatergoer can look anywhere on the stage at any actor, regardless of where the playwright intended the center of attention to be. Television viewers see only what the director wants them to see; they cannot see a speaker unless the camera is focused on that speaker. In the theater, voices and action tend to direct attention to the actors, but the audience still has a full view of the stage and can look wherever they choose.

The theater audience, remaining in a fixed location, sees the entire show from the same viewpoint. In a television show, the camera, which controls what the viewer sees, may look at the action first from a great distance, then with a tight close-up. It may photograph the actors from above the stage or from the far left side. It may focus on an actor's hands or right profile. While this selective view provided by the camera concentrates the viewer's attention on a specific area, it restricts the actors' freedom of movement. On stage, actors may vary their positions a step or two without seriously affecting the scene, but television actors must keep within camera range or the audience will lose sight of them. On one occasion, an actor seated on a bench during a tight close-up of his face rose suddenly to a standing position. The home viewers saw only the tight close-up of the Marine Corps symbol on his belt buckle until the director switched to another camera, which picked up the full view of the man.

This need to keep an actor's movements within camera range is so important that occasionally even professional performers rely on chalk marks on the floor to indicate their correct positions in relation to the camera. John R_____, a student playing the role of the stationmaster in Arnold Ridley's mystery thriller, *Ghost Train*, found it difficult to stay "in character" while remembering to adapt his stage crosses to the limits of camera range. During rehearsals, the director warned him, even threatened him, to move only as directed with no improvised sauntering around the acting area. During the telecast, John followed instructions and stood exactly in front of the ticket office door. However, he kept twitching his left shoulder and jerking his body at three-second intervals. These weird movements, completely out of character, distracted the studio audience and the home viewers, and drove the director to the verge of delirium. Not until after the telecast did the director learn the explanation for John's strange behavior. The filament in the especially constructed scoop light was water-cooled. A leak in the covering lens allowed hot water to drip rhythmically on John's shoulder, causing him to jerk at three-second intervals. However, he did stay within camera range, and the show went on!

Still another difference between television and the stage is provided by the television control room. The director of a play cannot communicate with the actors while they are on stage, so he or she must make all comments during rehearsals. The television director, however, can converse with the floor manager via the intercom, and the manager, in turn, can give instructions to the actors throughout the show. Directors can determine at any moment which of the characters' reactions they wish the audience to see.

Even the setting in a television play is different from the stage presentation. Television scenes can be changed instantly by focusing the camera on a different part of the studio where a scene has been set up in advance. A one-minute commercial allows adequate time to dolly the camera to another part of the set, as seen on *Saturday Night Live*. True, theaters have speeded up their set changes with lighting blackouts and skeleton set pieces—techniques adapted from films and television. However, the number of running feet (that is, distance from the extreme

Gilda Radner giving editorial comment on *Saturday Night Live.*

left to the extreme right) of scenery needed for a stage set is much greater than for television, and, therefore, stage sets are more expensive than the fractional sets used in a television studio.

Then, too, settings can be "faked" in television productions more easily than on the stage. Because the camera sees with one eye at a time, the viewer cannot judge the size of objects. A two-foot model of a park, for instance, appears as a full-size real park until a life-size finger points to an inch-high tree. A head-and-shoulders shot of a hunter with tree branches visible at the curve of his shoulders suggests the setting of an entire forest. To the camera—and thus to the viewer—a couple seated in a stationary canoe in front of a moving picture of lake waters and shoreline appears to be gliding through the water.

With the use of chroma key, an electronic process whereby a television performer stands in front of a blue or green background, film, videotape, or slides are inserted where the camera "sees" the blue or green in the original picture. This creates instant scenery. In television news, for example, a picture or film is often shown over the shoulder of the anchorperson. Behind the performer is a blue background. Another camera scans a picture on an easel, and where the blue appears on the

Jane Curtain spoofing television news on *Saturday Night Live*.

original camera, the viewer sees the picture coming from the second camera. Newscasters must be careful not to wear a blue coat or tie as the picture would also appear right through their clothing.

One of the most noticeable differences between stage and television production is the timing. The curtain rises on a school play at 8:15 Friday night. There are two ten-minute intermissions, and the final curtain falls at 10:20. On Saturday night, a snowstorm and a resulting traffic jam cause the opening curtain to be delayed five minutes while late arrivals are finding their seats. The Saturday night audience is the more responsive, applauding frequently and laughing at every attempt at humor. The final curtain comes down at 10:35, fifteen minutes later than on Friday night. A television program, on the other hand, is not interrupted by audience feedback. It begins at 8:31 (even if the audience hasn't tuned in yet), and the final commercial rings down the curtain at 8:59:30. Thus, the television actors have less freedom to ad-lib or to lengthen or shorten their pauses because of the exact timing required by the program schedule. Closed-circuit television within a school system, or even an educational broadcasting station, is less restricted by schedules than commercial networks, which feed programs over the line in split-second timing. An earthquake tremor in California which threw electric clocks off for only thirty seconds caused instant ulcers for network officials in New York as they waited half a minute for a program coming from the West Coast. Thirty seconds of silence and a blank screen are an eternity for a commercial network.

Choosing the Medium for the Message

The student who has a message to communicate needs to compare the audience, the setting, the time requirements, what can be seen and heard, and the movement required, in order to choose wisely between presenting his or her program on stage to a live audience or presenting it on television.

Why not radio?   It may be that radio, rather than television or the stage, is the best medium for what you want to get across. Although radio programs are subject to the same strict time scheduling as television, the radio show can transport the listener back and forth in time and space—certain sound effects suggest a scene in a factory; a few bars of music and a little imagination take the listener to the Orient in seven seconds. Radio was often called "theater of the mind" because listeners actually participated by creating the scene in their own minds. There are no props, no costumes, no make-up, and no scenery. The performer may use a script throughout the program. If the message can be conveyed through verbal clues alone, if it can be conveyed through words, sound effects, and music, then radio is a satisfactory medium. If, on the other hand, part of the message is conveyed by nonverbal clues, you will want to select television or the stage as the medium for your message. If a comedian's facial expressions and clumsy movements are his or her stock in trade, he or she selects television as appropriate for that brand of humor. If one picture is worth a thousand words, you need to consider the impact of a televised message that the mini-bike can do everything the motorcycle can do—and cheaper!

In certain areas, radio appears to be a more effective medium. Teachers of young children often find that radio stories stimulate a child's imagination and develop creativity more than television programs, even those specifically designed for children. An eighty-five-year-old seamstress who had never seen a baseball game in her life became an avid fan and quite knowledgeable about the fine points of strategy by following Chicago Cub games on the radio, assisted no doubt by the fact that radio sports-casters have to do more describing and explaining than television sportscasters. The radio play *Sorry, Wrong Number* by Lucille Fletcher, in which a woman overhears a cold-blooded murder being planned on the telephone, is an example of emotional impact and dramatic effectiveness carried only by sounds.

Another factor that might affect your choice of a medium for your message is the widespread use of radio today. Far from collapsing after the invention of television, radio is still a powerful means of communication. *Broadcast* magazine estimates there are over 8500 radio stations on the air, where there are only 950 television stations. Radio, however, has changed greatly to meet the demands of a new audience. FM, for example, was originally created for broadcasting classical music, because of its high fidelity and static-free reception. Today, many of the rock stations crowd the FM band, while AM radio broadcasts many all news or talk programs. Students carry their transistor radios to the beach, to the picnic grounds, to the student union, even to study centers—an indication of the large audience to which radio appeals. Even the car radio has become indispensable to home-bound commuters, who listen to traffic directions broadcast from a helicopter hovering above the expressways.

Not long ago, an eastern university received a complaint from students because the library was so quiet they couldn't study. They had gone through high school doing their homework to the accompaniment of music selected by radio's popular disc jockeys and had become conditioned to the noise of today's popular music. So the university piped recorded music into one of the library's soundproof rooms for those who needed music along with their reference books.

A recent survey of more than three hundred midwestern high school students showed that in winter they preferred television and in summer they spent more time listening to radio. A logical explanation of this preference is the declining quality of television programming during the summer months and the ease with which transistor radios can be carried to the beach and other outdoor spots.

Film and videotape.   No comparison or analysis of nonprint media is complete without reference to videotape or film. Before

A Minicam truck used by news crews of TV stations allows them to go anywhere. Notice the antenna on top, which sends the signal immediately back to the TV station.

Minicam crews can go almost anywhere with the new portable TV cameras.

portable video equipment, television depended on film for most of the "on the spot" news stories outside the studio. Film was smaller than the bulky video recorders and could record news events easily. However, film is not without its disadvantages, which encouraged stations to use tape when video became smaller. One of the problems with film was that it had to be physically transported from the news event, and it often took up to an hour to get the film back to the TV station. Then, of course, the film had to be processed and developed before it could be edited and used on the air. This took valuable time and prevented some good stories from getting on the newscast.

More and more, television is turning to videotape to record programs and news events. Early TV programs were almost always produced on film, but programs such as *All in the Family* changed that when some producers turned to tape.

Videotape has all but surpassed film for television news departments. With the new portable ENG (Electronic News Gathering) video recorders and "minicams," news teams can record a story on videotape and send the signal back to the station by the use of a microwave signal. Most TV newsrooms use a "minicam" van for news footage. On top of the truck is a large microwave antenna. An engineer beams the signal back to the station directly from the truck. This also allows the remote news crew to go "live" during the actual newscast from anywhere in the city. Videotape equipment and techniques have changed in the past few years, making television a dynamic media for news.

So if you choose television to put across your message, you are selecting a composite medium—one that combines techniques from theater, film, and radio; a highly technical medium used to produce artistic results; an impersonal, electronic instrument used by people to communicate with other people in a personal way.

Television, however, does not perform magic. A confused, unappealing sales pitch does not become persuasive merely by being televised. A dull, boring speech does not become exciting and stimulating just because we see it on television. The television medium carries the message from the sender to the receiver, but the medium must be used to its highest potential to achieve maximum effectiveness. With television you may be speaking to thousands of people at once, but it's important to remember you are speaking to only one or two people in one place. This *one-to-*

one communication makes television more personal than theater or a live performance. With its focus of attention, its personal one-to-one relationship, its visual emotional impact, its immediacy, and its mass appeal, television has its own techniques.

To communicate an idea effectively on television, you ignore none of the basic principles of communication. You must know what viewers are like; what their attitudes are; under what conditions they are viewing; what are their prejudices, emotions, goals; what knowledge they already have. You must appraise your message from the viewers' standpoint. What will it mean to them? How will they translate or decode it in terms of their own experiences and feelings? Then and only then are you ready to send that message by way of television.

If you have a message to get across to the majority of people in this country, television is your medium.

A Communication Model

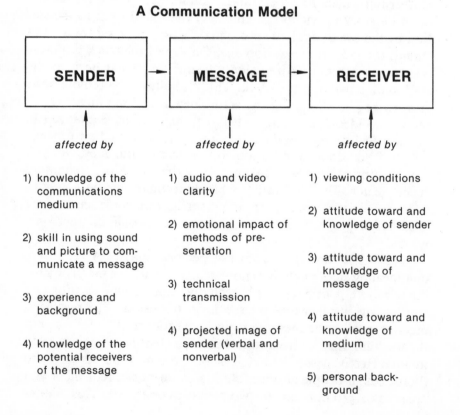

SENDER	MESSAGE	RECEIVER
affected by	*affected by*	*affected by*
1) knowledge of the communications medium	1) audio and video clarity	1) viewing conditions
2) skill in using sound and picture to communicate a message	2) emotional impact of methods of presentation	2) attitude toward and knowledge of sender
3) experience and background	3) technical transmission	3) attitude toward and knowledge of message
4) knowledge of the potential receivers of the message	4) projected image of sender (verbal and nonverbal)	4) attitude toward and knowledge of medium
		5) personal background

Put Them All Together They Spell Television

A is for Announcer, who always says, "Hi!"
    Then shows you the package and tells you to buy.

B is for Bunker, that lovable bigot.
    Some folks can't stand him, but even more dig it.

C is for Cigarettes, now off the air
    (A source of great comfort to Smokey the Bear).

D is for Detective
    They all seem defective.

E is for Election, that quadrennial race
    When even the loser puts on a good face.

F is for Films, a parade of great hits,
    Chopped and "adapted" in 12-minute bits.

G is for Game Show with prominent banners
    That identify all of those second bananners.

H is for Household, including your pet
    Who's included in surveys as "watching the set."

I is for Intrigue, domestic and foreign.
    The guys are like Bogey, the women like Lauren.

J is for Joke. If it's one that you know,
    The gag is a spin-off from some other show.

K is for Kiddies, who won't be deluded;
    They know that the batteries won't be included.

L is for Laugh Track, as complex as Bach
    For every slight sight gag, a thunderous yock.

M is for Migraine and Margarine and Mild.
    The products are bold and the promises wild.

N is for Nielsen—aye, there's the rub!
    Ever meet a "Nielsen family," bub?

O is for Option. It suddenly stops
    When the star or show has a rating that drops.

P is for Product, and selling's the game:
    The boxes are different, the contents the same.

Q is for Quiz Show, where riches await
    The contestant who knows his own name or the date.

R is for Repairman, who makes your heart stop
    When he says, "It'll have to go down to the shop."

S is for Sitcom, with insights astute:
    Daddy's a dum-dum, the Nazis were cute.

T   is for Talk Show, Yackety Yack.
    Yackety Yackety. We'll be right back.

U   is for Used-Up, a pretty good label
    For the stuff they stash in the re-run stable.

V   is for Vietnam, "the living room war,"
    Held over this season, with options galore.

W   is for Western, the home of the horse,
    Where the marshal is kind and the heroine's coarse.

X   is the brand with inferior flavor.
    To the rescue, then, comes the sponsor's lifesaver.

Y   is for Yawn, a reaction quite common
    In overviewed persons, both Herren and Damen.

Z   is for Zoltan or Zorach or Zlud—
    Those fiends on the Late Show, all thirsting for blood.
                    ROBERT LASSON and DAVID EYNON

Take Two

1. Select two or three of your favorite television shows and
    study them carefully the next few times you watch. Discuss
    with your classmates which of these programs would make
    good radio shows? Which shows depend on visual images?
    Could any of them be transferred successfully to the stage?

2. If any students have seen stage or club or concert ap-
    pearances by popular comedians, have them comment upon
    the performance. Then discuss the differences between the
    live performances and the same comedians performing on
    television.

3. Television frequently utilizes both classic and contemporary
    literature for programming. Watch a television production
    of a book you have read recently. Discuss the differences and
    the similarities. Be prepared to offer examples from the pro-
    gram you watched and the book you read.

4. Of the methods available for disseminating news
    (newspapers, radio, television), which do you prefer. What
    do you feel are the advantages and disadvantages to each of
    the media?

5. Using the communication model on page 34, discuss how this
    would apply to television. Who are the senders?

1. Tune in a *Monday Night Football* game that is being broadcast on both radio and television. Listen to one quarter from the television broadcast and another quarter by turning down the sound from the television and bringing up the sound from the radio. How do the sportscasters' play-by-play coverage differ from one medium to the other? Which do you think is more difficult to do? What kind of fill-in information or color does each use? Did the radio announcer keep up with the action as you saw it on television? Compare and analyze the differences and similarities between the two.

2. Watch a football game on TV, turn off the sound, and see if you can talk fast enough to keep up with the action as it happens. Make a list of fill-in information you could use during time-outs and between quarters and halftime. How could you devise a method of keeping all the players straight? What statistics should be kept so the viewer can keep up with the action?

    Try the same with a baseball game, which is slower. What is the difference in broadcasting a fast-paced event like football and a slower-paced one like baseball? How important is color information to a baseball game? Try to find information that could be used to fill dull moments such as the changing of pitchers.

3. Ask your school's athletic department if you could tape one of your school's basketball games play-by-play. Most schools will allow you to bring a tape recorder to record the action. Before the game, bring in background information on each team including records, injuries, last week's games, and styles of play. Plan a pre-game show for about five minutes before tip-off. Then, cover the game by giving a play-by-play description, as well as any color information you can use during time-outs. Perhaps you could find an interview during halftime. After the game, plan to "recap" by giving percentages, free-throw attempts, fouls, and mistakes.

Listen to the tape when finished to evaluate your performance on the air.

4. If you cannot record live during a game, ask one of the coaches to lend you a game film and try the play by play with the sound off. This will be more difficult, however, as game films are generally continuous action and usually leave no time in the film for time-outs and pauses. Who do you think has the more difficult role, the radio or television sportscaster? Why?

5. Plan a televised cooking or science demonstration that can be performed easily. Make a list of the ingredients or equipment needed and the steps in the process. Indicate which of these steps the viewer must see at close range in order to understand the process. At these points have the camera operator move in for a tight shot, or close-up (CU). As the class views the demonstrations, evaluate the clarity of the explanations and offer suggestions for improvement.

   Now perform the same demonstration without the camera, explaining on mike exactly how to follow the recipe or procedure. Discuss the major differences in the radio and the televised versions.

6. Prepare a one-minute radio commercial for one of these products.
   a. a toothpaste
   b. a soft drink
   c. a safety tire
   d. a stereo set
   e. a video recorder
   f. an airline
   g. a land development

   Using a tape recorder or radio studio equipment, create a straight radio commercial (one using no sound effects or music).

   Here are some suggestions for you to create an effective commercial.
   a. Keep your idea simple and to the point.
   b. Get the attention of your listeners immediately.
   c. Remember you are only talking to one person; imagine you are talking to someone.

d. Develop your commercial around some emotional appeal such as economy, safety, status, pride, or love.

A one-minute commercial is approximately 125 words depending on how fast you speak. Write and record the commercial to determine if you can "sell" your product. Remember to be enthusiastic and sincere.

7. Present the same commercial on television. Videotape the commercial to determine how your eye contact, gestures, and delivery help to sell the product. For television, you probably will have to memorize the script, because reading on camera is distracting and less effective.

8. Create a three-minute story on one roll of super 8 film with no sound. Remember that one roll of film is approximately three and one-third minutes. Plan to have credits with a title and performers in the beginning. The story should not have to depend on sound. Include the following types of shots in the film:

a. a wide shot
b. a medium shot
c. a close-up
d. a panning shot
e. a shot in which the camera moves.

Here are some topics for your film.
A Students' Day
Frustration (everything goes wrong)
After School Activities
Working on a Hobby
Washing a Car or Dog
Feelings (love, hate, happiness, or sadness)
First Time on Roller Skates
Remember that a film is not a one-shot wonder, but a series of shots that tell a story when they are put together. Plan your film completely before you start filming. Edit the film in the camera as you shoot rather than editing the film later, unless you have the capability of editing after shooting. Filming is different from television and should be carefully planned in advance.

9. Prepare a list of advantages and disadvantages of television as the medium for communicating a message. Be sure to indicate when the advantage or disadvantage may apply only to a specific circumstance or type of audience.

3

Visualizing the Message

If you want to communicate effectively, you must have a clear and unmistakable idea of what you want to get across and how you want them to respond. If you should ever want to communicate by television, you must also have a clear and unmistakable idea of what kind of visual images or pictures will make your message most meaningful to the viewer. As a telecommunicator, you would think of everything you wanted to say or do in terms of pictures; you would select, devise, and compose television pictures that would get the idea across without distracting the viewers' attention from the response you wish them to make to your message.

To achieve effective visual communication, you must know how to obtain television pictures that will tell the story, explain the idea, or sell the product. You should begin to think in terms of pictures rather than words to communicate your message. For example, let's imagine you are the director of a major league baseball game. It's the bottom of the ninth, and there are two outs. The clean-up man is up to bat. The score is tied at this point, and it's all up to the batter. This is a tense situation isn't it? Now, how could you show the tension of the game, especially that of the pitcher and the batter, with the pictures you are televising to the viewers? What shots would you put on the screen from your cameras on the field?

Perhaps you might get a close-up shot of the pitcher's face as he wipes the perspiration or shakes off the sign from the catcher; a medium shot as he uses the resin bag; a close-up of the batter's face as he stares down the pitcher; a close-up of the batter's hands as he fidgets with the bat; a long shot of the fans; a close-up of the dugout as everyone anticipates the first pitch.

These are pictures that tell a story when they are put together on the screen. That's your job—to create a visual impression used to communicate your message. Sure, you also have the audio or sound to help you, but it's the visual element that is important in television. Sometime, turn off the sound for a minute during a TV program and notice how much you know from just the pictures presented to you.

The television camera is the vehicle that must take you to this goal. Whether you drive a Cadillac or a jeep, certain common principles apply to the operation of a gasoline-powered motor vehicle. In television, too, there are certain basic principles that apply, regardless of the type and sophistication of your camera equipment. You must be functionally familiar with (1) the television camera, its lenses and its capabilities; (2) camera movement; (3) picture composition; (4) visuals, graphics, props; (5) scenery and background; (6) lighting and color, even for black and white television; and (7) special effects.

The Camera

The logical starting point as you begin to think with pictures is the television camera, which provides those pictures. There are two major kinds of television cameras in use today: color and monochrome (black and white).

Color. Most commercial television studios use color cameras today, as most homes have at least one color set. Because color adds a natural dimension that black-and-white images lack, it creates a positive psychological effect.

Early color cameras were large and cumbersome, and the quality of the color signal was marginal at best. They often used three-and-one-half or four-inch image orthicon pick-up tubes, which made the cameras large. A smaller, less expensive camera tube was created for the industrial market and schools. The cameras were smaller, rugged, and less expensive, but the picture was not as clear and needed much more light to get a good picture.

A new tube called a *lead oxide* or Plumbicon[1] tube was invented to replace the image orthicon cameras. The Plumbicon has the advantages of the smaller, more rugged vidicon tube, while surpassing it in picture quality and ability to get a good picture under lower lighting conditions.

There are many brands and kinds of color cameras on the market today. These range in price from about $800 for the color camera used in homes with the new video recorders to over $90,000 for some of the color cameras used by the networks for broadcast. Some use three separate Plumbicon tubes to pick up each primary color (red, blue, green for TV), and some use a series of dichroic (color separating) filters to place certain colors

Ikegami HL-79A ENG/EFP color TV camera

1.   Plumbicon is a registered trademark of the R.V. Phillips Co.

A color camera used in a closed circuit TV studio.

Ikegami HK-357A Microprocessor-controlled Field/Studio

on a certain part of the pick-up tube. These colors are put on one vidicon tube instead of three.

Monochrome.   Most schools still use black-and-white television cameras, although many are investing in color. Generally, black-and-white cameras are easier to operate than color cameras that need special lighting (to be discussed later), set up, and warm-up time. Whether black and white or color, the function of a television camera is the same; to change light (the scene) into electrical impulses that can be read, interpreted, amplified, transmitted, and decoded by your TV receiver.

Lenses

What the viewer sees on the screen depends on what the lens is picking up. Therefore, it is essential that you have a working knowledge of the effects achieved by different lenses and composition.

Focal length.   Older television cameras had turrets in front that had four different lenses ranging from a wide angle lens to provide shots of large groups, to a long close-up lens for far away shots. When a different lens was needed, the camera was taken off the air, and the camera operator moved the turret so a new lens was placed in front of the pick-up tube. This was time consuming and awkward. Now, all color and most black-and-white cameras use zoom lenses (often called variable focal length lenses).

One zoom lens can replace up to ten different lenses on the older turret cameras. The advantages of a zoom lens are obvious: 1) lenses can be changed while on the air by simply zooming in or out; 2) cameras become much smaller and more portable; and, 3) one lens can replace six or seven single focal length lenses. Zoom lenses, however, do not come without their disadvantages: 1) they are much more expensive than single lenses; 2) they usually need more light because there are elements inside for light to pass through; and, 3) the picture coming from a zoom lens is not as crisp or sharp as that from a single lens.

The principle of a zoom lens and a single focal length lens is the same. A zoom lens can become a short focal length lens (wide angle) by zooming out, or it can become a long focal length lens (telephoto) by zooming in. It is easy to remember. When you are zoomed out, you are using a wide angle lens, and when you are zoomed in, you are using a telephoto lens.

Some of the color cameras use an electronic "shot box" to preselect the speed and ratio of the zoom. Others use a manual crank on the side of the camera to zoom in or out. Still others might use a push rod under the camera to accomplish a zoom. When you are using a wide angle lens, you have a large field of view. The objects appear smaller, and you can move your subjects or the camera easily without refocusing. When you are using a telephoto lens, the field of view will be smaller, the objects will appear closer and larger, and the camera or the object must remain still or focusing will be a problem.

f stop.   In addition to focal length, lenses are also classified according to the amount of light they let into the camera. Since the amount of light entering the camera is the most important single element in taking the picture, this characteristic of the lens is an essential factor in the quality of the television picture. The iris diaphragm is the opening that can be made larger or smaller to regulate the amount of light admitted to the sensitive surface of the vidicon pick-up tube. The iris opening, generally called the f stop, is adjusted according to the amount of light you have on the set or on the object you are televising. The number of the f stop, marked on the lens ring, indicates the size of the iris opening. The lower the number, the wider the opening and, thus, the greater the amount of light entering the camera. In other words, the size of the f-stop number and the size of the lens opening are reversed. An f/3.8 lens would have a smaller opening than an f/2.5 lens. Vidicon lenses usually range from f/1.0 to f/22. A lens is considered "fast" when a great amount of light can enter even at a low f-stop number; a lens is considered "slow" when only a small amount of light can enter, even with a high f-stop number.

F/22

F/5.6

F/1.5

It is important to practice adjusting the lenses with different amounts of light to determine the best opening for a clear picture. If you have to open the lens very wide to get enough light, you will find it much harder to focus.

Depth of field.   In addition to the focal length of the lens and the speed of the lens, the two characteristics just described, a third factor affects the visual communication of your message: depth of field, or the area in which all objects at different distances from the camera are in focus at a single lens setting (See page 48).

The focal length of the lens, the iris opening, and the distance between the camera and the object affect the depth of field. For instance, there is greater depth of field in a long shot than in a close-up; therefore, there is greater freedom to move the camera and still keep the object in focus. Increasing the amount of light on an object is a simple way to increase the depth of field, because the iris opening does not have to be so wide.

The fact that objects not in the depth of field are out of focus can help or hinder the communication of the idea you want to convey. Backgrounds out of focus merely help the viewer concentrate his or her attention on objects in focus within the depth of field. This is called selective focus; where certain objects are in focus, and others are out of focus. Sometimes a director may

By carefully using a short depth of field, a director can select what is in and out of focus.

Notice with the use of the lense, the director can place either the student or the camera in focus.

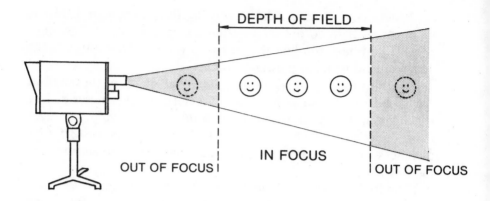

want to change this focus so that the scene in focus will now go out of focus, and the one in front of or behind the original scene will suddenly come into focus.

Imagine a television scene focused on a woman in the background with a telephone in the foreground out of focus. Suddenly the telephone rings, the woman's image goes out of focus, and the phone becomes sharp and clear. This is accomplished by having a short depth of field. The television viewer can concentrate better on a shot of the coach and benchwarmers at the side of the gym floor if the background of fans in the bleachers is out of focus, and the coach and benchwarmers are in focus within the depth of field. The greater the depth of field, the fewer problems you will have in focusing on a subject quite close to the camera and in focusing when the camera or a performer moves. The greater depth of field is easier for focusing and movement, but you will want to use a more shallow depth of field for variety and special effects.

The depth of field is controlled (1) by the focal length of the lenses—short lenses providing greater depth of field; (2) by the f-stop opening—smaller openings providing greater depth of field; and (3) by camera movement—the greater the distance between object and camera, the greater the depth of field.

The most practical way to acquire a working knowledge of depth of field is to practice with the camera in a lighted studio or classroom—moving the camera back and forth, adjusting the focus for a clear picture at each distance. If the floor space is small, try using shorter lenses. Have another student walk beside your camera for the first few tries, adjusting the lens opening as you move the camera and focus. *Remember that the viewer will see only what your camera sees, not what you see as you look over the top of the camera.*

Camera Movement

Another factor affecting visual communication is the movement of the camera. The support on which the camera is mounted is called a *dolly*. The dolly may consist of a central pedestal or a tripod. To *dolly in* means to move the camera and its mount, or dolly, closer to the subject; to *dolly out* means to move the camera and mount away from the subject. Commercial studios sometimes have crane dollies that permit the cameras to be elevated. Most school studios have dollies that, if they can be raised at all, are lifted by hydraulic pressure at the turn of a wheel or by changing the length of the tripod legs (though the latter process is too complicated to be attempted during a show). Often the director uses the cameras subjectively; the camera actually becomes a character. In a courtroom scene, for example, the de-

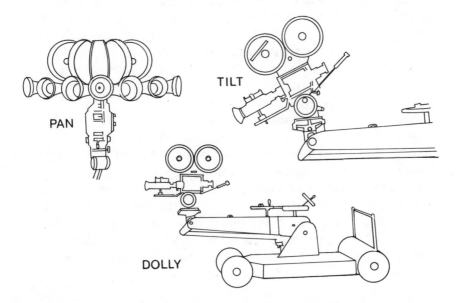

PAN

TILT

DOLLY

There are two basic types of mounting heads. The cradle head (below) balances the camera, even when it is tilted at an extreme angle, without having to be locked into position. The friction head (right) counterbalances the camera with a strong spring and has both a vertical and horizontal locking device.

fendant shouts, "Here he comes!" All the people look into the camera as it dollies down the aisle. Suddenly the camera becomes the central character, and we become the witness walking down the aisle to settle the court dispute.

You would dolly in to concentrate on a person's facial expression or to follow a performer moving toward the rear of the set, from the general to the specific. You would dolly in to achieve that effect in the courtroom scene. In a dolly-out, you would be moving from the detail to the overall. (If your studio or classroom has a wooden floor, the ridges between the boards will make smooth dollying extremely difficult.)

Pan means the horizontal movement of the camera from left to right or right to left while the pedestal or dolly remains stationary. It corresponds to turning your head left and right without moving your body. This camera movement, a shortened form of the word "panorama," is the one you would use in shooting across a row of singers or a chorus line of dancers. It can be used to follow a moving object or to show the association of several objects that have something in common, such as the expressions on a row of students' faces when a startling statement is made. When you pan past several objects, be sure there is not too much space between the objects. While you are focusing on an object, pan slowly; while you are between objects, pan faster.

Tilt refers to the up-and-down movement of the camera while the dolly remains stationary. It is the same as panning up or down and can be used for dramatic effects, such as panning *up* to make a person or object appear taller or higher or panning *down* to reveal the pot of gold at the base of the rainbow.

There are two basic types of mounting heads that permit you to pan and tilt the camera. One, the *cradle head*, balances the camera on the dolly even when the camera is tilted at an extreme angle. It does not have to be locked into position to hold the camera safely even if you have to walk away from the dolly. The other, the *friction head*, counter-balances the camera with a strong spring and has both a vertical and a horizontal locking device. This is the more commonly used head for small vidicon cameras.

Truck is the lateral movement of the camera and dolly to the left or right. It is an easy way to keep a laterally moving object in focus because it is always the same distance from the camera. To show a row of pictures from exactly the same angle, for instance, you could truck past them. If you were televising a swim meet, a pan would be insufficient because as the swimmers moved past the camera, you would not be able to tell who was in the lead. The camera would not be in a position to see who is in front. If you truck the camera as they swim, you could always determine who was in first place.

Truck and dolly, then, refer to movements of the camera and its dolly. *Tilt* and *pan* refer to movements of the camera while the dolly remains stationary. To make smooth transitions from one picture to another, so that the viewer can concentrate on the message without disturbing distractions, the camera operator must practice these four basic movements until they can be executed perfectly.

Even though a variety of pictures is essential for interest and sometimes for clarity, it is wise for inexperienced camera operators in a small studio to minimize the amount of camera movement. Place the cameras where they can take the maximum number of shots without bumping into set pieces, rolling over their own cables, or knocking down an auxiliary lighting standard.

Picture Composition

One of the best examples of effective framing and composition of a picture to communicate a message is the cartoon strip. Study the *Peanuts* cartoons, for instance, or *Wizard of Id, Nancy,* or *Doonesbury,* and notice how each frame makes a picture-statement. The following basic suggestions will help you arrange camera pictures, which will focus your viewers' attention on the message and communicate its meaning without confusion:

1. Use an "establishing shot," so called because it tells the viewers what the whole looks like before they see a part. An example would be a view of a discussion group around a table before a head-and-shoulders shot of one speaker.

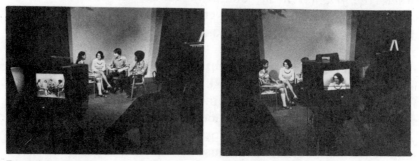

Establishing shot   Head and shoulder close-up

2. If you have two cameras and are shooting ad-lib (without a script), keep one camera on an establishing shot ready to show the entire situation. An example would be showing a view of the entire basketball floor with one camera, while the second follows a player down the court. This way, if you do not know what is going to happen next, you could get a shot of the entire action with a wide angle lens to be safe. This is called a *cover shot.* The general rule is, "When in trouble, go to cover."

3. Seat the speakers in such a way that their physical relationship represents their intellectual or emotional relationship. For example, have opposing political candidates sit on opposite sides of a table, making sure that the camera angle is such that the center of the picture framed by the camera is not a blank wall. Never separate people at opposite ends of the screen.

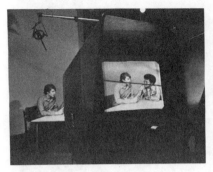

Good arrangement   Bad arrangement

4. A simple rule of thumb for framing two people during an interview is to have two or four shoulders visible, never three.

5. Try to frame your television pictures from a variety of angles instead of always directly in front.

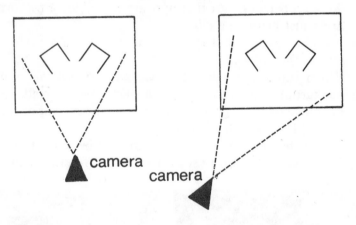

camera

camera

6. Another good rule: Normally the camera is at the eye level of the talent. Point the camera *down* on the subject to show weakness or inferiority. Shoot *upward* toward the subject to show strength or dominance. In the film *Citizen Kane*, every time the audience sees Kane, he is shown from a low angle to show his importance and power over people. The other characters are shot from high angles to make them appear less important. Often, a small child looking up at his or her parents would require a low angle shot to make the parents look larger.

Weakness   Strength

7. Avoid a camera shot that appears to cut off a performer's arms just below the elbows.

8. Avoid a camera shot that appears to cut off a performer's legs at the ankles.

9. When framing a picture, notice how the set pieces in the background are related to the performer. Avoid the appearance of ferns growing from a person's head or a lampstand bisecting a handshake.

10. Try to change from one picture to another at the time when the viewer will want to see something different because of a

Background should be related in order to avoid these kinds of shots.

thought change. In other words, compose a new picture at the end of a sentence, a paragraph, or at the end of one step in a demonstrated process.

11. The viewer should be able to see how each shot is related to the previous one. If the viewer sees a man knocking at the door, and the next shot shows him seated in a chair, the viewer is distracted from the story by wondering if the man walked, skipped, or staggered from the door to the chair.

12. The picture should show the viewer how the various props are related to the person using them. If a chef lifts a bottle of milk to measure out a cupful, the viewer needs to know where the bottle was when the chef picked it up, and where he or she got the cup. In other words, let the viewers see what they need to see to make the message clear, without distractions.

13. When two people are facing each other, a tight close-up shot of a profile should face the same direction as the person faced in the preceding picture.

14. When framing a tight close-up of a person's head, allow sufficient space at the bottom of the picture to enable him or her to look down without having his or her chin disappear from the picture.

15. Avoid a close-up that will distort an individual's appearance or emphasize physical defects.

16. In framing the picture for the camera, remember that 21 inches is probably the largest size screen available to most viewers; therefore, don't dry to crowd too much into any one frame.

17. Try to use the same aesthetic principles of balance, emphasis, and composition that you would use in nontelevised pictures.

This

Not this

18. When performers face to the right, place them a little to the left of the center of your picture. If facing left, place them a little to the right of center. Then they won't look as if they're facing the picture edge, preparatory to leaving.

19. Two people in a frame should be placed slightly diagonal to the camera rather than directly in front of, and parallel to, the bottom line of the picture as framed by the camera.

This   Better than   This

20. When performers cross from one place to another, keep the camera ahead of them as if pulling them in the direction they are going, rather than following them. (See sketch.)

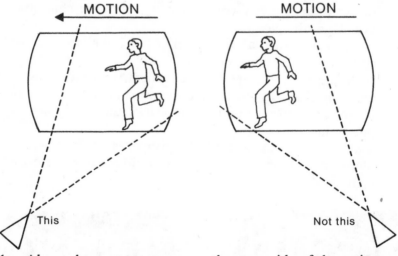

This   Not this

21. Always keep your camera on the same side of the action or the action will appear to be reversed. In a football game, keep all the cameras on one side of the field. If you are following a runner towards a goal and suddenly cut to a camera on the other side of the field, the runner will appear to have reversed direction.

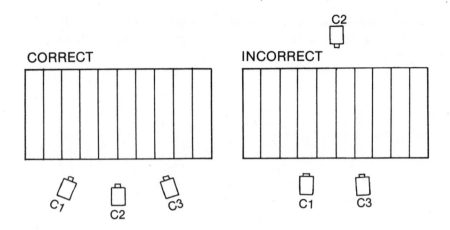

22. Try a variety of camera locations for shooting two or three people at a table.

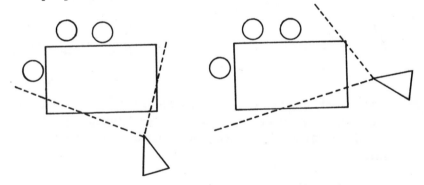

23. During actual production, you will not have more than a few seconds to compose television pictures. Therefore, you need to practice arranging props and people effectively until you have developed an "instant sensitivity" as to which pictures will communicate your message clearly and without distraction.

24. Because the two-dimensional television picture tends to be uninteresting, try to achieve a three-dimensional effect by giving attention to an object in the foreground and to the background of the picture.

25. Just as the student of a foreign language must learn to think and to dream in that language, so the television student must learn to think and dream in terms of picture-messages. As you plan a program, you compose pictures for ideas;

you frame pictures as a still photographer does with his or her hands. You don't think "ecology," you think "rubbish pile."

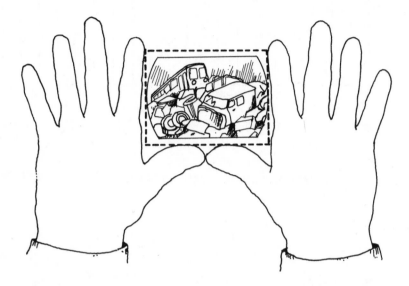

26.   Plan to set up a sequence of objects to be shot in the same location. For example, four weather forecasting cards should be arranged in sequence, so the camera can pan smoothly.

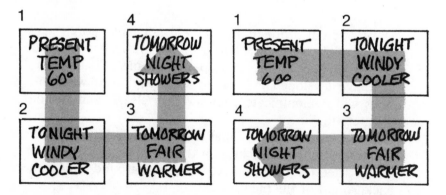

27.   Decide *how* to change your picture statements by changing from one camera to another. Cutting to another camera requires a reason. A director changes cameras to show a new subject or uses a close-up to emphasize a point. The director

does not change merely for variety. When changing to a new camera, here are a few suggestions to follow.

Suggestions for Cutting
a.   Good cutting goes unnoticed.
b.   Do not cut blindly for variety.
c.   Do not cut to a similar shot from another camera. There is no reason to cut if the other camera has essentially the same shot.
d.   Do not cut on a pan.
e.   Do not reverse the action in your cutting.
f.   Do not cut abruptly from a long shot to a close-up. Go to a medium shot first.
g.   Don't cut to extreme angles. A sudden cut to a person's profile may result in that same person looking entirely different.

When to Dissolve
a.   Dissolve to show that a change of time has taken place.
b.   Dissolve to show that there has been a change in place.
c.   Dissolve to things that are not anticipated. For example, dissolving to a woman wearing a unique hat during a baseball game surprises the audience.
d.   Dissolve when going to different media. For instance, dissolve when going from a slide, to live studio, or to a film, unless the slide or film has been given a verbal introduction.
e.   Dissolve to keep the flow of continuity. For example, during the performance of a ballad, you would go from a medium shot of the singer into a close-up. Some songs might require a cut at the end of each line of the song; others might require a dissolve when the ideas are not too clear.

When to Cut
a.   Cut to a close-up when you know where the person or object is in the preceding shot. If the talent is holding an object, cut to a close-up, don't dissolve.
b.   Cut to new objects or people when they have been introduced verbally.
c.   Most of the time, cuts are used. Remember that during a dissolve, the audience is temporarily confused.

Visuals: Two-Dimensional

Mastery of effective picture composition and correct camera work will not guarantee good television photography if the individual components of the picture are blurred, too bright, too crowded, too small, too large, too numerous, or too muddled. Therefore, one of the most obvious and frequently used "visuals" with which you must become familiar is the two-dimensional picture, photo, sign, poster, or label known as a "graphic."

Aspect ratio.   The first principle you need to know is that television pictures are always in a four (horizontal or across)-to-three (vertical or up-down) aspect ratio. That is, the ratio of the

VERTICAL MATERIAL

WILL APPEAR LIKE THIS   OR THIS

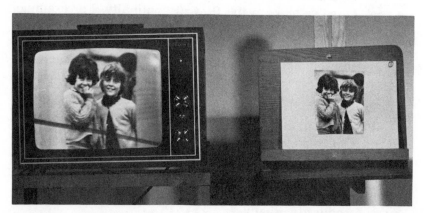

All graphic material should be in a 4 x 3 ratio. When original material is not in that proportion, artwork should be mounted on a card that is in that ratio, as in the case of the above.

width to the height will always be 4 × 3. The camera tube picks up and the receiver presents this rectangular composition. If you try to frame with a television camera a vertical picture whose proportions are 3 × 6, for instance, you will cut off the top and bottom, or you will show parts of the studio or classroom at the sides of the picture.

If it is impossible to obtain pictures, graphs, charts, etc., which are rectangular in a 4 × 3 ratio, mount them on a 4 × 3 card. It will be helpful if all graphics in any one production can be the same size, say 16″ × 12″, so that one camera adjustment can be used for all.

Borders. A second important principle in preparing and using graphics is known as the "rule of six." Since about ten percent of the picture you see on camera is lost in transmission to the receiver, it is important to compensate for this loss by leaving a border of unused space around the frame of each picture, sign, poster, notice, etc.

To determine the amount of space to be left in the border, the rule of six is used. Take a piece of cardboard the size of your graphics (16″ × 12″, for instance). Divide this area into six equal parts thus:

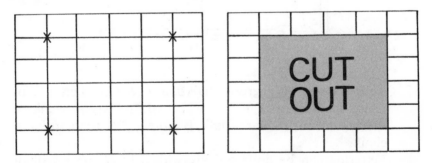

At the intersections of the lines nearest the edges mark an X and join these X's with a heavy line.

Cut out the part inside the heavy line. Use the remaining frame as a guide for any graphics you prepare. Lay it over a sign or other announcement, and keep all the letters within the cut-out area. Do the same thing with all pictures. Words or picture elements outside this center portion will not be visible on the television screen.

Here are some other basic principles that can guide you in preparing graphics for visual communication on television:

1. Use dark cards and letter them with light colors, rather than using light cards with dark or black letters.
2. Bear in mind that dull textures televise better than shiny, glazed, glossy surfaces.
3. Don't try to crowd more than three lines of lettering or writing on one graphic.
4. Number the graphics in the order in which they will be used.
5. Leave more space between letters and lines than you would leave in an off-camera sign.
6. If the lettering or writing is to be done on a chalkboard, the 4 × 3 ratio still applies. It is helpful to divide the chalkboard into a series of graphics.

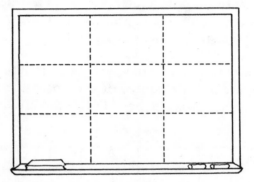

7. Yellow chalk on a green chalkboard televises better than white chalk on a regular blackboard. Television chalk, a special half-inch square chalk, is more legible than ordinary chalk.
8. Lettering can be done quickly with a brush or speedball pen, tracing the shape of letters through a stencil. Don't use freehand lettering unless you are a skilled artist and can make the letters look professional. Amateurish lettering on graphics can ruin an otherwise superior presentation.

   Most television stations now use a character generator, a typewriter that electronically inserts the letters on the TV screen. These can be incorporated into a computer and stored for retrieval during news broadcasts or during sports events.

ECONOMY NOTE: The classified section of a newspaper lettered with a flow pen can simulate a professionally prepared graphic.

This character generator by Vidifont keys lettering into the program.

9. Mount cut-out letters or press-type letters, which can be purchased with or without glue backing, on posterboard for truly professional-looking graphics.

10. Commercially prepared maps are usually cluttered with too many small items to be clear. If you want to use one, trace important areas with a felt-tip flow pen to darken the boundaries; or trace your own map, including only the areas to be discussed.

Visuals: Three-Dimensional

Properties and articles used in a telecast are also called visuals. (Some production centers, however, use the word *visual* for both graphics and three-dimensional objects.) Obviously the selection, placement, and use of visuals are of utmost importance in television, a medium in which effective communication requires more than "radio with pictures." If a visual will hold the viewers' attention and help them understand your message, use one—and use it correctly. If the visual is being included just in order to give them something to look at on the television screen, don't use it.

The satisfactory use of visuals in televising a message depends upon (1) the method of display; (2) the background against which the objects are seen, and (3) effective lighting. Each of these varies with the complexity of your equipment, but the principles are the same.

Display.   First, consider how to display the object. Show its size by placing it next to a human being, or next to an article the size of that is well known. If the object is to be operated or manipulated, try to have the camera face the object in the position of the manipulator or operator. The importance of the camera position, as far as the viewer is concerned, is illustrated by the difficulty a person encounters when trying to show someone how to tie a tie when the two are facing each other.

It is important not to obstruct the vision of the viewer. Use a pointer or a pencil to indicate the different parts of the object. If it is a small article, hold it on a firm surface like a table top instead of waving it about, making it impossible for the camera to focus on it. Any object will be more readily identified as to form and shape if it is viewed against a contrasting background and is correctly lighted. For example, dark liquids in a test tube should be displayed in front of a light background; light or clear liquids should have a dark background. One regular television performer who uses numerous chemical displays keeps available a piece of cardboard that is dark gray on one side and light gray on the other; this enables him to display clearly all types of liquids in test tubes and beakers.

To be sure the viewer's perception of the object is clear and unobstructed, it is sometimes advisable to fasten a mirror directly over the object and focus the camera on the reflected image. This kind of overhead shot is especially helpful, for example, when the

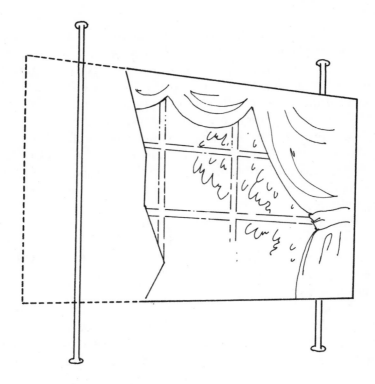

Extension poles used for lamps and towels make good "pole cats" if your studio ceilings are not too high.

viewer needs to see the position of the hands on a typewriter keyboard or the consistency of the ingredients in a mixing bowl.

An imaginative setting can provide interesting display areas as well as a contrasting background. "Pole cats" can be used to mount graphics on squares or rectangles of colorful materials and textures that contrast with the draperies or flat wall surfaces. Extension poles used for lamps and bathroom towels make good pole cats if your studio ceilings are not too high.

To provide these two essential visual elements—contrast with the background and an unobstructed view—certain set pieces, such as furniture, can be helpful. Furniture used by performers should be placed six feet or more away from the wall to permit the kind of backlighting that will outline the performer and the visuals, separating them from the background. Specially shaped tables and counters make it easier for cameras and lights to get closer to the subjects for a clearer view.

Occasionally, with some types of pictures, it may be necessary to use duplicate objects—one in a shot that shows a person handling the object; the other, properly displayed outside the playing area, in a tight close-up shot by a second camera. This duplication is especially helpful in televising coins, stamps, musical notes, library cards, footnotes, and the like.

A word of warning: any unobstructed, well-lighted interior shot may reveal sloppy production efforts: unpressed cloths, dirty surfaces, dusty table tops, wrinkled draperies, scaly paint, or daubs of dried paste. These betray the amateur and distract the viewer.

Settings do not have to be elaborate to be effective. Heavy, rough-textured draperies can be hung at the corner of a classroom to provide an interesting background and at the same time improve the acoustics by covering some of the hard reflecting surface of the wall.

Another interesting background can be made from window shades on which photomurals have been pasted or pictures painted. These shades can be raised and lowered to reveal settings appropriate for an individual speaker, newscaster, or commentator.

Lighting.   The most common problem in television photography, however, is proper lighting for effective visual communication. All sorts of unsuspected things can affect lighting. The glare from the chalk dust in the eraser tray can cause a distracting line across the screen. The shiny slats of a Venetian blind can cause streaking across the picture. The glare of lights reflected from a glossy photo print can cause "hot spots," or white light. Fluorescent lights may flicker and produce horizontal lines across the television picture. It may also cause the picture to have a greenish appearance because of the color temperature. (See page 69). Hound's-tooth patterned suits, as well as silk dresses, can reflect light and create what looks like heat waves shimmering upward from the bottom of the television screen. A person's nose can make a dark mustache-like shadow on the upper lip. The shoulders can reflect a bib-like shadow across the chest.

Cameras have their own idiosyncrasies in reacting to varying degrees of light. A commercial studio discovered this while televising a style show, when its camera #2 mysteriously transformed a black skirt with a white blouse into a white skirt with a black blouse. It is always a safe rule to check everything with your own cameras and your lights. Have the auditorium director or someone familiar with stage lights suggest what you can do with available equipment, for no camera and no performer can achieve visual clarity, much less effective communication, if the lighting is inadequate.

Bright lights are not the simple answer to lighting problems. A lighted area will appear bright only when there are dark tones present to contrast with it. If the faces of the performers do not appear bright enough (no pun intended!), merely adding more light may not help. The additional light will flatten out the facial features and will force the camera operator to "stop down" the lenses (close them to shut out light). A better solution may be to provide more contrast between the area behind the performer and the area in which he or she is standing by simply reducing background illumination. Conversely, too little light on a scene may obscure the picture with snowy specks called "noise."

To have the correct kind of light in the correct place is as important as to have the proper amount of light. The amount, or intensity, or level of light is measured in footcandles. Some light meters used by photographers are calibrated in footcandles, that is units for measuring light or illumination, just as sound is

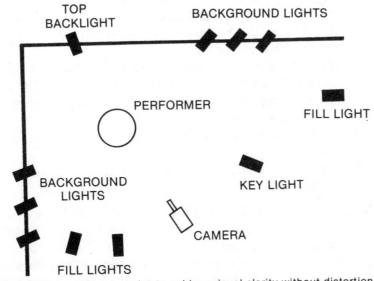

Use light from different angles to achieve visual clarity without distortion. The basic kinds of light are distinguished by the source or angle from which they illuminate the TV picture.

measured in decibels and weight is measured in pounds. Classrooms are usually lighted at levels varying from 40 to 75 footcandles. Approximately 200 to 250 footcandles are needed for vidicon cameras. Remember to check the cameras in your studio or classroom to determine the amount of light required by the peculiarities of your particular system.

The source of light is as important as its intensity. If all the light comes from directly above the head of a person, for instance, the frontal bones at the eyebrows will cast shadows on the eyes, the nose will cast shadows on the upper lip, and the chin will cast shadows on the neck. If all the light comes from below, equally distorting shadows will result. If the source of light is all at the front, people and objects tend to flatten into the background and lose the three-dimensional effect. You are familiar with the silhouette effect created by having all the light behind an object.

It is important, then, to use light from different angles to achieve visual clarity without distortion. The basic kinds of light, distinguished by the source or angle from which they illuminate the television picture, are as follows:

1. *Base* light: overall illumination of the area by instruments that spread the light, such as scoops.
2. *Back* light: illumination from back and above to form a rim around the head and shoulders of performers, making them stand out from the scenery in a three-dimensional effect, usually provided by spotlights.
3. *Front* or *key* light: aimed from the same direction as camera to produce highlights and shadows on the face of a performer, outlining the bridge of the nose, creating high spots on the forehead, cheekbones, and chin.
4. *Fill* light: used to reduce the extreme shadows caused by front lighting.
5. *Eye* light: a tiny spot mounted on or near the camera to throw light specifically on the face of the performer.

The amount and kind of lighting affect the way a black-and-white camera picks up colors. The viewer may see a man in a gray suit and a gray shirt. Actually, the man's suit is blue and the shirt is gray. A red cushion on a green sofa may appear to be the same color as the sofa. The size and shape of a pale blue object displayed against a royal blue background may not be dis-

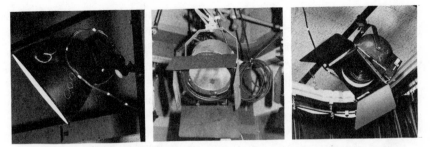

Lights are identified by the source or angle from which they illuminate the television picture: Base light, such as the scoop (left); back light, such as the spot (center); and fill light, where barndoors allow the operator to adjust as necessary (right).

tinguishable because there is no contrast between object and background on the viewer's television screen. Yet performers are told to avoid wearing black and white, a combination which would appear to give the best possible contrast. This is true with color as well.

These apparent contradictions are the result of the difference between the perception of the human eye and the pick-up capabilities of the television camera. The human eye can distinguish hundreds of shades between black and white; the television camera can differentiate among about ten. These contrasting degrees of color that the camera can pick up and the receiver can reproduce are called the "gray scale"; engineers use

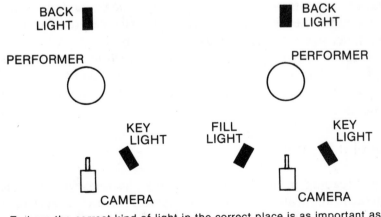

To have the correct kind of light in the correct place is as important as having the proper amount of light.

a chart of ten steps from television white to television black. A black-and-white television camera will show all colors as shades of gray. Extreme contrasts, such as television white #1 and television black #10, do not pick up well. The middle values, #2–#7, give the best production effects. A red dress that measures about #5 on the gray scale and a pink scarf that measures about #3 would provide a good contrast on the television screen, even though they might not be too pleasing to the eyes of someone in the studio. White uniforms cause more difficulty with contrasts than pale blue ones. Pink, light green, yellow, and tan all photograph as the same light tone on the gray scale, about #2. Again, remember to check colors with *your* cameras and *your* lights and *your* background materials.

To provide appropriate contrast for visual clarity, the color of a performer's clothes should not be too near the color of his or her skin. Make-up, in which the face is slightly darker than street make-up, can be used to accentuate this difference. The basic principles of stage make-up—to cover perspiration sheen, to hide wrinkles, to highlight bone structure, to mask the blotchy appearance of a dark beard, and to frame the eyes for emphaphasis—apply in television as well. In *The Selling of the President, 1968*, author Joe McGinnis tells of Richard Nixon's problem in television appearances, and of the need to have handkerchiefs soaked in witch hazel ready to absorb the shiny perspiration from his face whenever the camera was turned away from him.

In the early days of television all performers used a whitish pancake make-up and a dark liner on eyes and lips, to provide adequate contrast for a satisfactory camera pick-up. Today, modern cameras do not require heavy make-up, and most performers require little, if any. True, some people with dark skins may require highlights of tinted make-up; or men may occasionally need to hide shiny bald spots or to darken skin that photographs lighter. Most women will use make-up a little heavier and darker than the kind they normally wear.

Special Effects

The foregoing principles of visualizing the message have their practical application in various special effects that can be achieved with film and certain types of equipment available in most schools.

Films and slides.
1. The 4 × 3 size ratio applies to any films or slides you may want to show in your televised presentation.
2. In slides, the contrasts must be sharp and clear, especially in color slides.
3. Most 16mm film was not made for the 21″ television screen. When reduced from a projected 9′ image to a 20″ image, much of the definition is lost.
4. You must get specific permission to use films or parts of films on television. It is not sufficient that your school has rented a film to be shown on a projector in classrooms. In addition, most films are copyrighted and require permission to televise. This is true even if you own the print of the film. Televising the film requires a special license from the film producer.
5. A sound film can be used only if the film itself was shot at sound speed. However, you can show it as a silent film and add your own commentary.
6. Do not try live pick-up of slides, filmstrips, or moving picture films by a studio camera. If the room is dark enough for clear projection of the film, the chances are that it will be too dark for adequate camera pick-up, the film will be too washed out. Unless you have a film chain that can be operated from a separate control room, you will be wise not to include film in your televised production.
7. If you do have a film chain, a multiplexer will increase the flexibility of your system. The multiplexer is a mirror arrangement in which pictures shown by two projectors can be picked up by one camera. For instance, you can alternate slides on one projector with 16mm film clips on the other projector and pick up both with camera #2 while you are on camera #1 giving a commentary.

Rear-screen projection.   Another special effect that uses film is rear-screen projection. This film requires special equipment, but the variety of scenic background it provides makes it well worth the cost. In rear-screen projection, slides are projected through a translucent screen by a projector behind the screen. The image is picked up from the opposite side of the screen by a studio camera. For example, a slide picturing a map of Europe can furnish the background for a newscaster reporting the latest conference in Paris.

A multiplexer is a mirror arrangement in which pictures shown by two projectors can be picked by one camera.

The expression "super" refers to one picture being superimposed on another. In this case, NBC's John Chancellor is shown with a picture of France being superimposed in the background. Two cameras and switching equipment are required in this technique.

The "Green screen" technique allows anchorpeople like ABC's Frank Reynolds to talk to correspondents in other areas of the country or world.

A man standing in front of such a screen in a studio can appear to be outdoors under a row of cherry blossoms, which is projected from a colored slide behind the screen. A news reporter can appear to be standing in front of the Capitol in Washington because he or she is standing in front of a screen on which a slide of the Capitol has been projected from the rear of the screen.

Super. If you have two cameras and switching equipment, you will want to use the "super." Two pictures are transmitted simultaneously, one superimposed on the other. A man's name appears at the bottom of the screen showing his head and shoulders. One camera is shooting him; the second camera is shooting a black card with his name in white letters near the bottom.

Key. Many special effects generators allow you to key two cameras, which looks better than a super. For a key, one camera is focused on a black tagboard with white or yellow letters, the other camera is focused on the scene being televised. When the key switch is thrown, the white letters are electronically inserted into the scene. This has the advantage over a super in that it does not diminish the illumination of the original scene.

Here is the shot as seen on the monitor from camera 1.

Camera 2 picks up a close-up of the set.

By inserting a key, the graphics on camera 2 are electronically placed on the screen over the picture on camera 1.

Special effects economies. Not all special effects are expensive, nor do they all require special equipment. Lay-ons of dark colors on a light flannel board (flannelboards are familiar equipment in many classrooms) provide an effective visual. The lay-ons should have sandpaper glued on the back to make sure they will adhere to the flannelboard, which should be in the 4 × 3 ratio.

The turntable of a record player makes an impressive display table for an object you want the audience to view from all sides.

A wooden frame 24″ × 18″, with picture-frame slides or quarter-rounds makes an ideal framework for graphics, covered by pull-outs which you can move with tabs.

This same principle used with pull-off masking tape can give the effect of a graph moving as you remove the tape from the rear of the chart.

ECONOMY NOTE: With the aid of your industrial or technical arts department or stage crew you can build some visual devices that will add variety to your television presentations. For example, an endless roll-up can be made from an old washing machine ringer. A crawl or title drum can be made from a 25-pound round carton in which laundry detergent is packaged.

All these principles of achieving effective visual communication with black-and-white cameras are subject to certain changes if you are fortunate enough to afford color equipment. Color origination is more expensive because the equipment itself is more expensive, including the color receivers. It is more com-

A crawl or title can be made from a 25-pound round carton in which laundry detergent is packaged.

plicated and requires more technical assistance from engineering staff members and more attention to details of costumes and setting. For studio lights, it requires quartz iodine lamps instead of the incandescent type. The color temperature (relative reddishness or bluishness of light measured in degrees of Kelvin) of most television cameras is set for 3200° Kelvin. Light under 3200°, like a flourescent light, will appear green; and light over 3200°, such as the sun, will appear reddish. Color television is becoming less complicated and expensive. New one-gun vidicon cameras are bringing more and more color studios to schools.

Television is a *visual* medium. You cannot expect the viewer, accustomed to watching commercial television, to accept uncritically a series of ill-conceived, inadequately lighted, poorly composed television pictures simply because they are being picked up by a school camera and being transmitted by a student crew. If television is worth doing at all, the picture must be good!

Take Two

1. What is meant by a "picture statement?" Why is it important to think in terms of picture statements?

2. Name two situations in which television directors would want a shallow depth of field in a shot. Explain what could be done to achieve a shallow depth of field.

3. Zoom lenses are more practical than a single focal length lens, but there are disadvantages. Discuss three of them.

4. Give an example of a situation in a television production when a director would use a subjective shot in the production.

5. Why is it important to keep the camera at the eye level of the performer? Discuss situations when you might want the camera higher than the performer.

6. Why is it important for one to know about aspect ratio for television?

7. Name the function of the following types of lights on a television set:
   a. key light   b. fill light   c. back light   d. base light

Three projects typify the problems and techniques of visual communication: video collage, commercial, and demonstration. Although only one project is suggested, it will be helpful to televise as many as you can.

Video Collage
What are you trying to learn?
1. How to begin in terms of picture statements.
2. How to communicate with television.

Instructions:
1. Pick a modern song with lyrics that are easily understood by everyone. Bring in a good recording of the song.

2. Write a script for each line of the song so that you can follow each separate idea contained in each line.

3. Find pictures that show each idea in each line within the song. Mount these pictures on cardboard or tagboard. Check for aspect ratio, and make certain they are large enough.

4. Divide the pictures and place them in front of two cameras.

5. Play the music for the audio, and choose the pictures in front of the cameras to match that line of the song.

6. If the song is fast paced, cut from one picture to another. If it is slower, dissolve from one picture to another.

7. Videotape the project. The audio will come from the recording, and the video will reflect the ideas in each line.

8. Use your imagination. Let the viewers see your interpretation of the song through your use of visuals.

Commercials
What are you trying to learn?
1. How to communicate ideas by way of a camera.

2. How to use persuasive appeals to influence others to act in a certain way.

Length: 1 minute

Visuals: Use a minimum of two. One must be a graphic (two-dimensional sign).

Subject: Do *not* copy a television commercial. You may use the same ideas or methods, but you must change the product. What you are selling may be real or fictitious. You may exaggerate the methods of used-car salesmen; the circus-type barker; the housewife testifying to the wonders of soap, fruit juice, and hair spray; the buyer who has suddenly become popular because of his or her chewing gum, hair color, shaving lotion, or toothpaste. Be as creative as you wish, as long as you show good taste and do not offend anyone.

Content: Make sure your message includes the fundamental human appeals—to self-preservation, property, power, duty, reputation, affection, physical attraction, love for family, and taste. Check a speech textbook if you do not know how a salesperson appeals to the fundamental drives that motivate people to act.

Effectiveness: Have other students in the class assess your effectiveness and suggest buyers to whom your presentation would appeal.

Production principles:

1. If you use brand-name products, cover the name with a label bearing a fictitious name in letters large enough to be clear and neat enough to look professional.
2. If you use actual food products, check them on camera. Raw meat often looks more appetizing than cooked meat. Onions need a little food coloring. Real poached eggs may not look as appetizing as half a peach inverted on a crustless slice of bread.
3. Hold the product still long enough for camera to focus clearly on it.
4. Check the lighting on your product. It doesn't matter what *you* look like (or does it?), but the product must look good!
5. Display the product against a contrasting background, so its shape can be easily distinguished. (How will a frisbee look against your plaid shirt?)
6. Information that is easy to forget (advertisers' phone numbers, prices, addresses) should be lettered neatly on a

graphic even though you plan to give it orally, too.

7. Time is a worrisome problem. Which is worse, to have time run out before you tell us where we can buy the product, or to stand there with "egg on your face," in silent terror, for the final 15 seconds? Solution: Have a "cushion" of music, or signs, or object displays that you can put in or leave out to adjust time variations. Perhaps you could have a logo or a nice display of the product that you could dissolve to at the end. This would serve as a pad at the end of the commercial.

8. Use your imagination. Be creative. Don't let viewers turn to another channel while you are selling your product. A student demonstrated the effectiveness of a liquid plant food by pouring a few drops on a wilted vine, which immediately shot up 24 inches (done with an invisible wire pulled by an accomplice hidden behind the drapes).

9. Check your own effectiveness. Would you buy this product if all you knew about it was what the viewer will see on your television presentation?

Demonstration

What are you trying to learn?

1. How to organize for clear understanding.
2. How to communicate ideas by way of a camera.

Length: 3 minutes

Visuals: One required

Subject: Select a process that you can demonstrate in three minutes. It should not be as complicated as a steam engine or have as many parts as a chess set. The process should be one that you know thoroughly and in which your classmates may be expected to have some interest. The following are only suggestions and are not meant to limit your creativity or imagination:

How to keep score in bowling
How to set a timer for turning lights on and off
How to kick a soccer ball
How to embroider with a tube of paint
How to serve in tennis
How to tie a halfhitch
How to play a chord on a guitar
How to peel an orange
How to shave a balloon
How to apply eye shadow

How to sharpen an electric razor
How to use a cookie mix
How to put on a lifejacket
How to do a card trick
How to park a car
How to use a cassette recorder
How to make a banana split

Production principles:
1. Remember to check every prop and every movement on camera for lighting, contrast, focus, placement.
2. If you're making something, have the finished product on hand. You can hide a cake in the file cabinet and pull it out of this "oven" to finish your demonstration of cake-making.
3. Don't let your hands hide what the audience needs to see. Turn articles toward the camera. Point with pencil or finger if your hands get in the way.
4. Keep display surfaces clear of extra objects or background objects that will detract from a clear view of your process.
5. Plan carefully where the camera will be. If you are showing stances for golf, will the camera have to tilt up to your face, pan over to a chart, tilt down to your grip, up to your face, down to your feet? What order is best?
6. If you have to move objects, move them slowly enough so that the camera can stay in focus.
7. If you're cooking, have you checked *on camera* the articles you will use? Does yellow Spry look as real as white Crisco?
8. If you must lift an object, brace your hand or arm on a table or counter. Otherwise you may tremble, or the object may be too heavy to stay in focus.
9. Plan what you'll do if things don't work. Always be ready with an alternative—just in case.
10. Have a running commentary ready for any lengthy process. While you open the can or container, say something.
11. Plan carefully a logical order for the demonstration. Don't confuse the viewer by inserting, "Oh, I should have told you. . . ."

There is an old saying that can be applied to your demonstration: "An order that can be misunderstood will be misunderstood—by somebody." Is your demonstration so clear that it can't be misunderstood?

4

Sounding the Message

The next time you watch a rerun of your favorite television program, turn off the sound and see how much of the show you can understand and enjoy. If that doesn't confuse you, try watching the used-car commercials during the late movie with the sound turned off. Can you imagine a telecast of a concert without sound?

A neatly lettered graphic appears on a silent picture tube, "We have temporarily lost the audio portion of this program. Please stand by." Or in your own studio, have you watched a student crawl on his or her stomach across the floor, inching out of camera range toward a fellow student who has forgotten his or her microphone? Each of these instances is a reminder that television is sound as well as picture.

Sound Sources

In television, as in radio, the sound consists of speech, music, and sound effects. However, the sound source in television is often in motion, as the singer or speaker moves about the stage or across the studio floor. Whereas in radio, the sound is positioned at a stationary microphone, even for special effects. Moreover, in radio the performer "addresses" (that is, directs his or her words toward) the microphone, but in television the performer addresses the camera. Microphones in television move about the studio to keep up with the action and remain out of camera range. Microphones in radio stay in their positions, but the performers move on and off mike.

Characteristics of Microphones

In both radio and television, it is necessary to know the characteristics and capabilities of the microphones you will have available for your use. One difference is an obvious one that you can see without knowing the technical characteristics—the way the microphone is "mounted" for your use.

Mounting.
1. *On a floor stand.* The *floor stand mike* can be used only when it is appropriate for the mike to be seen, never during a dramatic presentation. It cannot be used during a dance number or any other activity in which floor vibrations could interfere with good pick-up. It is often used for featuring certain sections of an orchestra.

   Inexperienced performers tend to kick the base of a floor stand or grip the center shaft and rock the entire instrument back and forth. If you are recording country music in Nashville, using special electronic effects, you may want to grab the microphone, but such a grip is not standard procedure in a television studio.
2. *On a table stand.* The *table stand mike* is convenient for panelists or other speakers seated around a table. A disadvantage is that it picks up the sound of drumming fingers or pencils on the table top. It is not effective when it must be

The floor stand mike can only be used when it is appropriate for the mike to be seen. For example, it should never be used during a dramatic presentation or any other kind of program where it would be obtrusive or out of place.

The table stand mike is convenient for panel discussions and similar types of programs.

passed around or shoved back and forth along the top of the table. It provides a good way to mask notes or a script, but the rattling of cards or sheets of paper against its base can be quite distracting. A felt table covering can prevent some of the disturbing noises picked up by this type of microphone.

3. *On a gooseneck.* The *gooseneck mike* is used with a floor stand or table stand. The mike itself is mounted on a flexible extension that enables users to bend the supports toward them or away from them as they wish the mike distance to vary.

4. *On a lavaliere cord.* The *lavaliere mike* has a cord (named after a lady's necklace) that permits users to wear the mike around their necks, freeing both their hands and giving them more flexibility of movement about the set. It can be hidden easily, but it is likely to pick up noise by rubbing against buttons, tie clasps, and the like. Users must avoid being too close to it when they bow their heads to read something or when looking down at something they are demonstrating.

5. *On the lapel.* This mike is clamped to the lapel of the coat. It is easily hidden from view and has the same advantages and problems as the lavaliere mike. Hiding the lapel mike underneath clothing tends to muffle the sound. A college science teacher who had rehearsed his television program in his shirtsleeves did not discover until the telecast that his lapel mike picked up an annoying static produced by his coat sleeve rubbing against the front of his wool jacket as he wrote on the board. Both lavaliere and lapel mikes give the user more freedom of movement than the floor stand, table, or gooseneck, but at the same time they present problems— the dangling mike cord that the performer must avoid tripping over; keeping away from the camera dolly; and getting tangled up in set furniture.

6. *In the hand.* The *hand mike* is especially good for outdoor interviews, like man-on-the-street programs. The interviewer can hold the mike close enough to the mouth of the speaker for a good pick-up, in spite of street or other extraneous noises. The hand mike has the disadvantage of keeping one of the performer's hands tied up and is thus unsuitable for a demonstration. A hand mike can also be clamped into a floor stand (like the one in the illustration). Thus, it can be lifted out of the clamp when performers wish to move about

The gooseneck mike can be used either with a floor stand or table stand. Its flexible mounting allows a speaker to vary mike distance with relative ease.

The lavaliere mike is worn around the neck, freeing both hands to give the speaker more flexibility in movement.

The hand mike is especially good for on-the-spot interviews and demonstrations. Clamped to a floor mike, as in this illustration, it allows the speaker to free both hands when necessary.

with the mike in their hands, or become stationary again during another part of their presentation, such as a musical number. Inexperienced performers are likely to wave a hand mike around like a baton, swinging it to and from the mouth. This can drive audio engineers to distraction, as they try to "ride gain" on volume that varies from one extreme to the other. To achieve a fairly even volume level during a telecast, the engineer must constantly manipulate the controls to allow approximately the same amount of sound to pass through at all times. These volume controls are called *faders*, *mixers*, *gain controls*, or *pots*, and the process of controlling the amount of volume is called *riding gain*.

7. *On a pipe or extension pole from the ceiling.* The mike permanently mounted in this way is sometimes referred to as a *bing* mike. It is especially good for musical groups, such as choirs, which remain in the same position throughout the telecast, or for any group where the sound source is immobile. A mike hung from overhead has other advantages. There are no mike cables on the floor; there are no shadows cast by the boom; no operator is needed to move it about; and it is easier to keep out of the picture, as the camera operator isn't likely to be shooting upward. Its disadvantage is that it must be kept high to remain out of the picture, and, therefore, may be too far away to pick up well, without extraneous noise. If the mounting is too high, there is likely to be a reverberation from studio or classroom walls. On the other hand, the absence of a floor cable makes moving the camera much easier.

8. *On an extension rod overhead.* The so-called *boom mike* is one of the most flexible of all microphones used in television, but it does require more floor space and one more studio crew member to move it about and adjust it as needed. The operator of the boom mike can raise, lower, pan, retract, extend, or rotate the microphone to keep it just above and in front of the performer. He or she must be careful to keep the boom mike in front of the sound source. Commercial studios usually have space for four-wheeled boom platforms that give the entire assembly a steadier base and more flexibility to move the mike 360°. Most school studios, however, have to be satisfied with the "giraffe" boom, a tripod frame with a narrower wheel base, moving on three casters. The boom

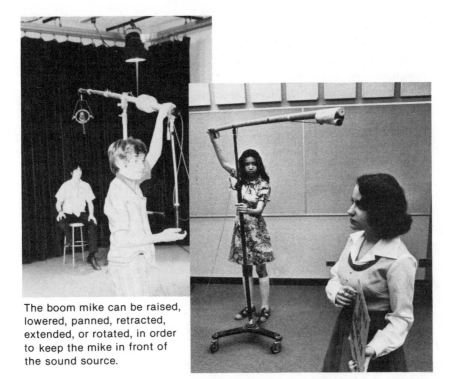

The boom mike can be raised, lowered, panned, retracted, extended, or rotated, in order to keep the mike in front of the sound source.

The boom mike is one of the most flexible microphones used in television, but it requires much floor space and one more studio crew member to operate it. The boom mike in this photograph is a do-it-yourself model.

mike creates problems for the camera operator because of its shadows; and also for performers, who must telegraph their anticipated movements to the boom operator in order to avoid getting hit in the head with the mike when they stand up. Some camera operators tie a two-inch long white ribbon to the bottom of the mike to warn them that the boom mike is beginning to be visible at the top of their picture frame. Then they can tilt down in time to avoid getting the boom mike in the picture.

ECONOMY NOTE. If you can't afford to buy a boom mike mount, you can make a satisfactory substitute by fastening a hand mike to a heavy pole.

9. *On the body: FM wireless microphone.* The *wireless mike* is really a small transmitting station concealed on the wearer's body. Although it is expensive, it is especially desirable in musicals or in outdoor presentations where stringing long cables is impractical. In many television newsrooms, wireless microphones are used so that the anchorpeople can walk over to the weather reporters or feature reporters. The anchorpeople are not tied down to desks by microphone cables. The microphones are attached to small FM transmitters located somewhere on the talent. Receivers are located in the control room and process the signals into the audio control boards.

Pick-up.

You can refer to a microphone, then, by the way it is mounted, such as boom mike, lavaliere mike, hand mike, etc. Microphones are also classified according to the direction from which they pick up sound. These differences are not always visible. The five common types are classified thus.

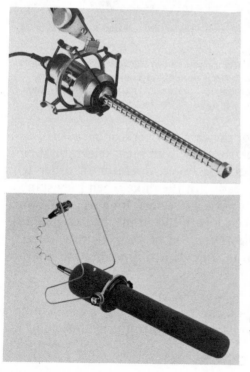

Two common types of microphones: On the left are shown two types of polydirectional mikes. The one above has a versatile range for use on a boom; the one below has a wide pickup range. The mike above is a unidirectional multi-purpose model that is commonly used for interviews.

1. *Nondirectional.* The *nondirectional mike* picks up the sound from any and all sides in a circular pattern around the mike. Usually its pick-up range has a distance limit and requires the main sound source to be within 10 to 12 inches. Obviously, it is a convenient mike to use with a group of several people, since it picks up equally well from all sides. However, this same characteristic makes it susceptible to all kinds of distracting background noises. It would not make a good microphone to put on a boom for television because it might pick up unwanted sounds of camera operators and the rest of the stage crew as well.

2. *Unidirectional.* The *unidirectional mike* picks up sound from only one side. Sounds from the opposite side are deemphasized or reduced; sounds from the sides of the mike are virtually wiped out. A performer using a unidirectional mike can stand farther away from it, as much as 14 or 15 inches, but cannot stand off to one side. This is the microphone used most frequently in radio stations, because unwanted noises are kept at a minimum.

3. *Bidirectional.* The *bidirectional mike*, as its name implies, has two live, or pick-up sides and two dead sides. It has been standard equipment in radio's dramatic shows, but is not very practical for the television studio. If two actors face each other from the live sides of a bidirectional mike, one of them must have his or her back to the camera. Furthermore, the mike will be visible in the picture.

4. *Polydirectional.* The prefix *poly* indicates that this is a many-sided microphone. The *polydirectional mike* is equipped with an adjustment screw for changing it from one pick-up pattern to another. By turning the screw, you can change it from unidirectional to bidirectional or from nondirectional to unidirectional. Its versatility makes it a practical, though expensive, mike to use.

5. *Cardioid.* Most new microphones utilize a *cardioid* or heart-shaped pattern. These microphones can be used for more than one person. This mike has eliminated much of the feedback problems (when a microphone is near a speaker and a high-pitched squeal is heard).

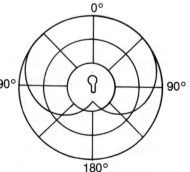

0°

90°   90°

180°

Frequency range.
Thus far you have been introduced to two characteristics of microphones; the way they are mounted, and their pick-up pattern. The third characteristic, and one of the most important, is the range of frequencies (high and low tones) that a mike can pick up. Since television sound is broadcast by the frequency modulation method, it is necessary to have equipment of high fidelity that will respond to and reproduce sounds of widely differing pitch. Frequency modulation refers to a technical change in the radio wave carrying the sound. Broadcasting that uses FM (as it is called) is characterized by freedom from static and more faithful reproduction of sound.

The one basic function of a microphone is to change sound into electrical impulses. Most microphones have two elements; a diaphragm, used to vibrate in accordance to pressure changes in sound, and, a generating element, used to change these sounds into electrical energy. In broadcasting, three types of microphones are used, but the effect is essentially the same.

Dynamic.
The dynamic type of microphone is perhaps the most popular microphone used in broadcasting. The microphone has a diaphragm attached to a metal coil located near a magnet. When a person speaks, the diaphragm vibrates. As it moves to and from the metal coil, a voltage is produced and varies as the diaphragm moves.

The dynamic mike is rugged, great for outdoor "remote" programs, and resists distortion. Although the frequency response is not as good as in some recording studios for music, it meets the needs of the radio and television stations that do not broadcast live music.

Ribbon.
Ribbon, or velocity microphones, are very similar to dynamic microphones except that instead of using a metal diaphragm, a very thin metal foil serves as the diaphragm and coil. The ribbon microphone is more sensitive and has a slightly higher frequency response used for musical recordings.

It does have its disadvantages for radio and television productions, however. It cannot be used outdoors, because the slightest wind will sound like a tornado. It cannot be used on a boom for television, because it will sound like wind as the boom is moved.

Great care must be taken not to misuse or drop the microphone.

Condensor.
The condensor microphone works on the same principle as the dynamic microphone, except that the backplate is fixed. An electric current, supplied by a separate power supply (usually a battery), changes the capacitance. As the diaphragm moves with changes in air pressure, the voltage is changed. Many television stations use this type of microphone as lavalier mikes for newspeople. Music recording studios often use condensor microphones because of their excellent frequency response.

The frequency range of microphones may seem like a problem only for engineers, and this is true of some studies with large staffs. However, in other television setups, student crews will have the responsibility for selecting and setting up mikes for a program. If a script calls for both speech and music to be picked up by one microphone, you will need to know which mike has a wide range of frequencies, to obtain the best pick-up. If a mike is to be used only by an announcer in a separate room called an "announce-booth," you will want the mike that is best for a voice pick-up coming from only one direction. Even expensive, sophisticated recording equipment cannot produce good music from a pick-up by a cheap mike with a low frequency range.

Acoustics

Another factor affecting the sound of your televised message is the acoustics of the studio or classroom in which your program originates. In other words, how clearly can sounds be heard or transmitted in it. Some sound waves pass directly into the microphones; other sounds are reflected off walls, floor, ceiling, windows, chalkboard, and other flat surfaces (such as counters with formica tops). When the walls are far away from the mike, there will be an echo effect. To control the length of time it takes any sound to bounce off the wall and back into the mike, studios have irregular wall surfaces, draperies, and wood or composition panels. The most flexible studios have both live (reflecting-sound) areas and dead (absorbing-sound) areas, which can be adjusted to regulate the amount of reverberation. A practical student once explained live and dead areas by saying that studios need to sound both "zing" and "kerplunk."

Out-of-doors sound, because there is no restraining space, is "dead," or, in the words of the student, "kerplunk." A room with considerable reverberation of sound, bouncing from one hard surface to another, is considered "live," or "zing." A studio is deadened by heavy draperies and carpeting. It is made live by exposing plaster walls and hard, shiny surfaces. In a classroom, a wood floor, plaster walls, and large window and chalkboard areas cause the sound to have a hollow or echolike tone. The brilliance and timbre of music and speech tones would be removed, however, if all the walls, floor, and ceiling were covered with absorbent surfaces. So you need to experiment with window shades, rugs, drop cloths, felt cloths, and screens until you achieve the best balance for the tone you wish to produce. You don't expect an interview recorded in the locker room to sound like a concert in the auditorium, but neither do you expect an oboe solo to sound like a leaky showerhead.

The number of people in the studio can affect the amount of sound that is absorbed. Each person represents the acoustical equivalent of about 4.6 square feet of absorbent material. Make at least one check of the sound quality when the studio has the people, the flats, and the material it will have during the telecast. If you rehearse in a classroom full of students and then record the program after school in an empty room, don't expect the same tones to be picked up by the microphone.

This acoustical problem can be illustrated by the story of a broadcast series by a famous symphony orchestra. At dress rehearsals, the studio engineer and the conductor were both pleased with the tone quality. Yet invariably, the actual broadcasts were less satisfactory, although all the audio controls and mikes were adusted in the same way. No explanation could be found until someone recalled that during the actual broadcast there was a studio audience. The front rows were filled with wealthy old men with starched dress shirts and shiny bald heads, which provided sound-reflecting surfaces the engineers had not taken into account.

The Performer's Use of the Microphone

The final and most variable factor affecting the sound of a television program is the performer. The public address mike in the auditorium, in the gym, or in the stadium is used to project the speaker's voice to large groups of people, sitting together, reacting as a group, in an audience situation. The microphone in the television studio is used to carry the speaker's voice to large numbers of people, too, but they are listening in small groups or individually in a more or less homelike environment. The ability to speak directly, as if talking with one individual, is as necessary for a successful television performer as the ability to look "through the camera lens to the viewer sitting in an easy chair in front of his or her television set.

Furthermore, microphones neither transform sloppy articulation into clearly enunciated speech, nor do they add variety and vitality to monotonous, deadly voice patterns. However, microphones do call attention to *s*, *ch*, *sh*, and similar sibilant sounds. To avoid these and other hazards, the inexperienced performer may find the following suggestions helpful:

1. When you are testing a microphone to get the proper level for the audio engineer, never tap or blow into the microphone. If you are using a ribbon microphone, you can cause damage to the metal ribbon by tapping it. Never test the mike by saying, "Testing 1-2-3." Test the mike by reading the first lines of the script. Then there won't be any surprises for the engineer when you start.

2. Practice "swallowing" *s*, *ch*, and *sh* sounds and concentrating on the vowel that follows each one, so as to avoid sending a narrow stream of air from your lips into the microphone. Concentrate on the *gra* in *grass*, the *all* in *shall*, and the *ne* in *happiness*. Pronounce *statistics* "stay-TIH-sticks."

3. Check with the technicians on the correct distance between you and the specific mike being used. Then stay there; don't be a creeper (edging to and from the mike) or a weaver (rocking from side to side). If you get too far away, the volume will have to be turned up. In addition to your voice, the listener may hear the piano pedals or the rumble of the camera dolly trucking across the floor.

4. Don't rattle script pages against the mike stand or on a table top. Remember that rattling paper is used to simulate the sound of a forest fire or rain on the roof.

5. Don't hit the mike stand with your feet or bang against the top with your hand.

6. *Never* whisper a cue or direction or question to another performer. You cannot hide anything from a mike that is turned on.
7. Don't hold the mike too close to your mouth. It will pick up little puffs of air when you pronounce words beginning with *p* and make them sound like shots from a BB gun. A whistle will sound like a mild explosion and can actually injure some sensitive mikes. A mike held too close will pick up breathiness, lip smacking, tongue clacking, swallowing, and occasionally even a heart flutter.
8. Be ever aware of the sound of your total presentation. It is as important as the picture. Don't ignore that microphone!

Communicating by Sound Alone: Performing on Radio

You can get the clearest impression of the images sound can convey by studying radio programs—how they are presented and what techniques are used to enable them to excite the imagination and translate auditory impulses into characters and situations as definite and real as any you see on television. You may be familiar with radio news, music programs, and an occasional weather report or emergency message, but most of you are less knowledgeable about radio drama and the old-time comedy and variety shows your grandparents enjoyed.

Voice of the radio performer. The radio performer has to do with his or her voice alone what the television performer does with the assistance of settings, costumes, properties, make-up, graphics, visuals, and observable movements. The radio actor, for instance, has to put his or her mood (not visible in a frown) and various bits of stage business (stroking the chin thoughtfully) into the lines. If these are not conveyed by the words, by the way the lines are spoken, they don't exist at all. The audience cannot see the performer listening to another character. The performer can indicate that he or she has been listening only by the response to the other person's lines. When someone being interviewed on radio concludes an anecdote with the comment, "It was the most frightening experience of my life," we are a bit suspicious of the listening concentration of the interviewer who merely answers, "Is that so! And when did you become interested in the migrations of birds?'' However, if the interviewer follows up the anecdote with a question like, ''After such a terrifying experience, did you ever go back again?'' we feel he or she has been listening attentively and reacting to the comments of the interviewee.

Positions at the mike.   The radio actor does have a mike and a script, and he or she must know how to use the mike from five basic positions: (1) on mike; (2) off mike; (3) fading in; (4) fading out; and (5) from behind a door, wall, or other obstruction. In general, when speaking on mike, an actor stands 12 to 18 inches away from it and uses enough volume to address a person four feet away. The sound perspective must be maintained. If the actor says, ''I must leave to catch my bus,'' he or she should back off while reading the line. If an angry mob is moving into the scene, their shouts should become louder as the group steps closer and closer to the mike. Fading in and out are as important as on and off mike.

The cast of a radio play usually gathers around two or three standing microphones, but a small cast of two or three may be seated at a table. Usually, actors prefer to be standing to ''get in the mood'' by performing actions suited to the words. Because the body responds as a whole, performers know their voices will sound more tense and excited if their bodies are tense and they are moving their legs up and down as if pacing with impatience. A radio director once had trouble getting the lovers in a tender scene to use the proper tone of voice. After he moved them to the same microphone, where they stood physically close together, it

A radio actor or actress must always be aware of cues from the director or technicians. Too often, inexperienced actors and actresses keep their eyes so glued to the script, they miss important cues.

was easier for them to display an affectionate intimacy in their vocal tones. Helen Hayes, playing the role of nurse Florence Nightingale in a radio show, held the script in her left hand while she stroked her left arm as if she were caressing a wounded soldier. In a radio presentation, action and feeling must be readily discernible in the tone of voice. The audience, seeing nothing, must hear all.

Reading the script.   These special techniques for using the voice effectively to communicate meaning and feeling in radio are complemented by equally important techniques in using the script to advantage. The fact that radio performers can read the script and don't have to memorize it, as one would do for television, is an important aid. However, it is also the downfall of inexperienced performers who sound as if they are reading and keep their eyes so "glued" to the script that they miss helpful cues from the director or the technicians.

Experienced, skilled radio speakers memorize the script almost as completely as if they were going to deliver it from memory. At rehearsals they mark their scripts, encircling or underlining each of their cues. They mark time-cues in the margins so they will know where they should be reading one minute before the close of the show. Descriptive comments (such as "as if frightened at the thought") are added to help interpret meanings to the listener. Radio speakers slide each page of the script quietly beneath the others after reading them, and are careful not to hold the script as a sound barrier between themselves and the mike. They watch for cues from the director and follow directions for special effects produced by the technical and sound effects crew.

Nonverbal cues.   Although each director creates his or her own nonverbal cues for communicating with radio performers, certain cues have become so standardized that they are used in both radio and television.

1. *Stand by.* This signal, which consists of raising the arm above the head with the forefinger pointing upward, warns the participants that it is almost time for a cue to be given, alerting them to be ready to perform on cue.
2. *Cue to start.* This is the go-ahead signal to execute whatever is supposed to be done or said at a particular time. It consists of pointing the finger at the person who is supposed to perform the action. It must be a clear, direct movement. When

Each cue must be clear and direct. In this example of the cue to start, notice how the finger is pointed directly at the person being cued.

the arm is already upraised in the "stand by" position, it is merely lowered to a horizontal position, the finger pointing directly at the person being cued. Curved fingers, waving limply back and forth, only serve to confuse the performer.

3. *Speed up.* Rotating the index finger clockwise is an indication that the director wishes the performer to speed up the tempo. If the director rotates the finger slowly, the speaker is to increase the speed just a little. If the director rotates his or her finger fast, the speaker knows the time is running out fast and the lines should be said much faster.

4. *Slow down.* Directors move their hands from a together position to an apart position, as if stretching rubber bands or elastic, thus telling the performer to "stretch it out."

To request a slower tempo, the director moves her hands from a together position to an apart position as if she were stretching rubber bands or elastic. In this example, the director is telling the performer to "stretch it out."

5. *More volume or less volume.* More volume is requested by extending the arm with the palm upward and raising the hand slowly or quickly to indicate how much more volume is needed. Less volume is indicated by extending the arm with the palm turned down and dropping the hand quickly or slowly.

6. *Move closer* to the microphone or *move back* from the microphone. To make this request, directors place their hands in front of their faces—with the palm inward to indicate moving closer to the mike and the palm turned outward to indicate moving away from it.

7. *Time cue.* The director holds up fingers to indicate the number of minutes remaining.

Here, the director is giving a time cue indicating that four minutes remain.

An upraised fist with fingers toward the talent is the signal to "wrap it up."

The signal to stop or cut is indicated by drawing the index finger slowly across the throat.

8. *Wrap it up.* An upraised fist with fingers toward the talent is a signal to close the discussion as quickly as possible.

9. *Cut.* The signal to stop is indicated by drawing the index finger slowly across the throat.

As you will learn in Chapter 5, "Transmitting the Message," the television director relays the directions for the speaker, via an intercom system, to the studio floor manager, who in turn signals the performer in a variety of ways. In radio, the director signals the performer with hand signals, such as the nine just described, and by facial expressions and other nonverbal cues. In television, the sound must be consistent with what is seen on camera and is complementary to what is seen. In radio, however, the sound must rely on its own effectiveness to create a visual image in the mind of the listener.

Take Two

1. Were silent movies really silent? Discover by reading or by talking to someone who saw these movies in a theater how they were shown.

2. Decide what microphone mounting would be most appropriate for the situations listed below. Be prepared to discuss the reasons for your choices.
   a. a kitchen demonstration of carving a turkey
   b. a panel of politicians and environmentalists discussing conservation
   c. a podium address given by a corporation president to a large audience of employees
   d. an on-the-street opinion poll
   e. a large choir concert given in a small auditorium
   f. on-the-scene commentary and description of a slalom ski competition

3. Discuss with your classmates the various types of microphone pick-up. Describe one situation where each type would be most appropriate.

4. Analyze the acoustical features of your gymnasium, auditorium, and library.

1. Sound effects

Sound-effects records can be purchased. Or sound effects can be created with your own equipment and recorded on tapes and cassettes. Or sound effects can be operated manually—a method that requires greater effort and imagination and ingenuity, but will enable you to cue more accurately and blend the sounds more realistically into the script. Before you begin presenting radio shows, try to reproduce the following sound effects, record them on audio tape, and then play them back to check how real they sound.

a.   *Raindrops*—Drop rice on the head of a drum.

b.   *Tap dancing*—Beat out the time with drumsticks on a folded newspaper, or hold shoes in your hands and tap them on a board near the mike.

c.   *Roar of a plane*—Hold a stiff blotter against electric fan blades, or hold an electric toothbrush against the palm of your hand.

d.   *Fire*—Crackle cellophane or crush onionskin paper near the mike.

e.   *Breaking bones*—Chew candy mints or celery close to the mike.

f.   *Gunshots*—Snap a ruler against the side of a cardboard box.

g.   *Telephone voice*—Hold the open end of a drinking glass to the side of your mouth while talking. (Normally it is done with a filter microphone.)

h.   *Monkeys*—Rub wet cork against bottle.

ECONOMY NOTE: If your school has no filter mikes or echo chambers, try some of these inexpensive makeshifts to achieve special effects like ghosts, or telephone voices. Hold the open end of a large drinking glass at the mike in such a way that you direct your words into the top of the glass and the mike at the same time. Or cover your head and the mike with a large metal wastebasket. Or speak into the big end of a megaphone with the small end toward the mike.

A cartridge recorder will automatically cue music and commercials.

2. Reels, Records, Cassettes

For music in a show, compare the advantages and disadvantages of using cassettes, reels of audio tape, records, and broadcast cartridge machines. Until recently open-reel tapes have had the best tone, especially for music, but nobody likes the chore of threading the tape.

Most radio and television stations today rely on broadcast cartridge recorders for music, sound effects, and commercials. A cartridge recorder utilizes a "cart" with a continuous loop of tape in predetermined lengths (5 sec, 10 sec, 20 sec, etc.). The advantage of a cartridge recorder is that the tape or cart is cued to a precise spot by the use of a 1000 Hz tone put on at the beginning of the program material. The recorder automatically stops when it reaches that tone and is ready for the next play. Most radio stations now transfer their records to carts as well as their commercials. The tapes do not warp, do not become scratched, and eliminate cueing.

If you don't need to start the recording at an exact spot or cue, you can take the lazy man's way out and simply slide a cassette into the playback. If you have an inexperienced sound crew, with one member who is always pushing the wrong button and erasing the tape, you will be grateful for this ingenious feature of the cassette. On the back of each cassette are two cavities, covered by plastic tabs. If you break off those tabs, you can't record or erase the tapes until you tape over the hole again.

a. Put a record and record-player, a reel of tape and a recorder, a cassette and a cassette playback out on a table. Now see which one you can load and bring up to correct volume the fastest. Check how long it takes you to find an exact spot on each of the three. Which seems best for a disc jockey? As background music for a story? Why is the record not so good for theme music that will be repeated at the beginning and end of each show for a week?

b. In preparation for a radio show, see how accurately and exactly you can "spot" a record—that is, locate a single measure of music at which you can begin playing without a "wooooo-ow" or a three-second warm-up. To "spot" a record, use chalk or colored wax pencil to cover four or five grooves in the general area you desire to fix accurately. Let the needle etch a clean line through the chalked area across the "spot" you want to play. Set the needle down on the clean spot and start the turntable to warm up to full speed, but hold the record to keep it from turning with the turntable. On cue, release the record and turn up the volume simultaneously. With practice you can become so proficient that you can release the record on a specific chord that you want to be the first audible sound—but it will take practice!

It is more difficult to cue or spot a record than to play a cassette or audio tape. However, this is more accurate than relying on the counter-numbering system of most playback machines, since the amount of leader tape wound around the take-up reel varies as much as an inch or more each time the tape is rewound. Marking the reel tape with a colored wax pencil will enable you to observe visually when the "spot" approaches the playback head, but this is not as accurate as spotting a record unless you are experienced. One tape editor was so proficient in locating even syllables of words that he was able to add "ing" to the final syllable of each "goin'," "wishin'," "thinkin'," "hopin'" in the speech of his somewhat inarticulate employer. However, most of you will not have his experience and skill.

3. **Radio shows**
With the ability to put sound effects and music on tape and cassettes, with music on records and tapes, with live, manually-operated instruments ready, try a radio show of your own. Have another student record your three-minute presentation of one of the following and play it back for you.

a. *A disc jockey show*—Limit the records to one minute so that you will have time for a two-minute introduction. Plan carefully how the music will be played. Do you want it to fade out under your voice? To stop abruptly? What will be your transition between records? Will you have an opening and closing theme? Will all records be by one group or one composer? Will all be on one theme? Will you interview one of the recording artists? Will you "plug" one of the records?

b. *A news-weather-sports presentation*—An important part of your preparation will be to determine the answers to these questions: What can you do in three minutes? What portion of the time will be news? Will the intended audience determine how much time will be devoted to sports? Will you have a musical theme? How will you make the transition between the parts of the show? Will you use the sound of a teletype? Will your speech tempo and tone of voice be the same for news, weather, and sports? Will you want the reports recorded elsewhere by another voice? If so, how will you play that tape and cue it in? Will you use a recorded interview for part of the sports segment? How can you make these recorded passages clear and distinct to the listener? How much local news will you include?

c. *Editorial comment*—Pretend you are the radio station manager giving an editorial comment on freedom of the press, the construction of a new highway through the city, the vandalism of shopping malls, the need for a civic auditorium, or some other matter of local concern. How will you command attention and keep your script from sounding as if you were reading it? If listeners turn to another station, your cause is lost!

d. *Commercials*—Commercials play an important part in the broadcast industry. Sometimes as much money is spent on the commercial itself, as on the program it sponsors. There are basically three types of commercials you may want to produce; straight, voice overs, and situations.

The easiest commercial to produce is a one-minute straight commercial using no sound effects or music. A one-minute commercial is approximately 125 words. Try to be as sincere and conversational as possible. It is a good idea to plan the commercial around one of the universal appeals that will hold the listeners' attention. Some of the appeals used by advertisers include love for your family, physical attraction, pride, and saving money. Pick a product, decide what appeal you will use to capture and hold attention, write, and deliver the commercial on tape. Listen to the tape to determine how effective you were in selling the product. Did *you* believe in what you were saying? Did it sound natural or more like words from a sheet of paper?

Music plays an important part in many radio commercials. It sets the mood for the entire commercial. A fast-paced commercial will use fast-paced music. Usually instrumental music is used rather than a vocal arrangement, unless it is a jingle written for that product. Write a commercial, and use music for the background. One important suggestion—don't use music that everyone recognizes. It might be a mistake to use "Staying Alive" from *Saturday Night Fever* because the listener may be tempted to listen to the music rather than the commercial. Bring the music up at the beginning, hold it, then fade it under your voice during the delivery (check the levels), fade it up at the end, and fade it out. Listen to the music. How effective was the music in the production? Did it add to the effect or detract from your presentation?

Many advertising agencies use humorous situations to capture and hold the attention of the listeners for radio advertising. Remember the first time you heard those zany *Time Magazine* commercials by Dick Orkin? They use characterizations, sound effects, and music to sell the product. This is the most difficult commercial to produce because it uses all aspects of radio production: voice, music, and sound effects. Write and produce a commercial utilizing a situation. For this commercial you should include an announcer, two actors, music, and at least one sound effect. Use your classmates to help you create a situation commercial. Here is a commercial created by one high school student for this assignment.

MUSIC: UP, HOLD, AND UNDER

ANNOUNCER: Now let's visit Ralph and Marge in their home discussing business.

RALPH: I'd better get that upstairs heating system fixed, not to mention those basement steps.

MARGE: Yeah, you should. Someone could freeze on the second floor and fall through those stairs.

SOUND: KNOCK ON DOOR, OPENS, THEN CLOSES

INSPECTOR: I'm the building inspector. Do you have a building permit for your home remodeling?

RALPH: Well, I uh. . . .

INSPECTOR: Just as I thought. I'll have to look upstairs to see if everything is in order.

RALPH: I wouldn't do that if I were you.

INSPECTOR: Nobody tells me what to do. I'll open that door if I want to.

SOUND: DOOR OPENS, BLIZZARD IS HEARD, THEN A SCREAM AND DOOR SHUTS

INSPECTOR: AHHHHHHH! That's cold. You've got a heating violation coming, and I'm not even to the basement yet.

RALPH: Please don't go down there, I'm begging you.

INSPECTOR: What's the matter, you got something to hide?

MARGE: No, he doesn't, but you'll be sorry if you go down there.

INSPECTOR: Hah, You're trying to scare me, but it won't work. I'm opening this
           door.

SOUND EFFECTS: DOOR OPENS, BODY FALLS DOWN STEPS, THEN A SCREAM

MARGE: At least he didn't land in the sewer drain.

SOUND: SPLASH FOLLOWED BY A SCREAM

INSPECTOR: (OFF MIKE) I'll sue you for everything you've got. You won't have a
           thing left.

MARGE: Big deal. My husband can always get a loan from Helpful Finance.

RALPH: That's right. I can always count on getting some help from the friendly
           people at Helpful Finance for a remodeling loan to an emergency loan.
           They'll listen to my problems, and I can pay back in 48 easy in-
           stallments.

 INSPECTOR:(OFF MIKE) Yeah, all right. But could you do something about those
           crocodiles?

BOTH: (IN UNISON) Crocodiles?

ANNOUNCER: Any one of our 57 Helpful Finance offices have nice, friendly people
           that you would really like to take home with you, but you can't because
           we make them stay here so they can solve your money problems faster.
           Some can even get rid of your crocodiles, too.

MUSIC: UP, HOLD, UNDER

                          by ERIC SZAMBARIS, student THORNTON TOWNSHIP HIGH SCHOOL

e. *Recipes or household hints*—Present a program of cooking recipes or hints for homemakers. Since your audience can't see what you're doing, how will you make
your directions clear? What is the proper tempo for dic-
tating a recipe? How can sound effects help? Will the
sound of beating six egg whites differ from the sound of
beating one egg white? Will there be a sound for a
"pinch" of salt? What about music?

f. *Play-by-play*—Give your imagination a workout by presenting an on-the-spot play-by-play of a horse race, a
stock car race, a hundred-yard dash, or some other
sports event. How much background sound should be
included with your voice, for atmosphere? Will you in-

clude a remote recording of an interview with a participant? Will someone introduce you? From what vantage
point will you watch the event?

Before attempting one of the group experiences in
communicating by sound alone, you will find it most
helpful to listen to a daytime radio serial, a radio play, or
a variety show. Because one person can play several parts
in a radio show by changing his or her voice and manner,
it will be possible for a group of four or five students to
present a radio play requiring a sizable cast.

1. For your first radio group presentation, don't try to
use an original script. Use a collection like *Plays
from Radio.* (See Additional Resources on page
116.) Some libraries have collections of radio script.
Let members of your group take turns being responsible for creating sound effects, making the opening
and closing announcements, and directing the show
by giving the cues.

2. After listening to the playbacks of your group's
radio shows, try your hand at writing your own
"soap opera," the name given to daytime serials on
radio. Write a takeoff, or parody, on one of the
famous radio shows of the past. If we had no television today, what kind of daytime serial would grip
the attention of the homemaker of the 1980s? How
about a contemporary switch to a story for the man
who stays home with the baby while his wife goes to
work?

4. **From radio to television**
Your group is now ready to experience sound for radio as
compared with sound for television. Pretend your disc
jockey shows on radio have just been given a lucrative television contract. If there are four in your group, present four
three-minute television shows using the same records you
used in your radio programs. How must you change them to
adapt them to television? What will people see? Will the
viewer see the technician or you rolling the tape or spinning
the platter? Will the source of the sound ever be seen? Will
the viewer see dancers, or musicians, or still pictures? Will he

or she see the group that made the recording? How much will you have to change the script to make it suitable for television?

Suppose you have been made public relations/publicity chairperson of the United Fund drive, the new band-uniform drive, the muscular dystrophy fund drive, the budget ticket sales, or some other worthwhile project for which you have been given a one-minute spot on both radio and television. You have "one minute of sound" to promote or sell your project to the radio listener. Don't waste a second of it with a trite beginning like "Thank you for letting us come into your living room tonight." Make every sound count for every second.

After you've heard and criticized the playback of your radio promotion, try a one-minute television plug for your campaign. Again, make every sound count for every second. What visuals will be most convincing in persuading viewers to contribute to your cause? Which is more effective, a few visuals that they see long enough to affect their emotions, or a bombardment of many pictures that blast away at their consciousness?

The old Chinese proverb, "One picture is worth a thousand words," did not mention sounds. Music and sound effects as a background to establish the mood for words can have an emotional impact. The sound track on a movie sometimes becomes as famous as the movie—for example, *Born Free* or *Saturday Night Fever.* Have two or three students from the oral interpretation or English class read aloud brief selections from either poetry or prose that describe a setting or a mood. Provide appropriate mood music and sounds as background for the reading. Does the sound assist the reader in creating the mood? Is the sound distracting? Is it too loud or too soft? Repeat the reading and observe the reader through the viewfinder of a television camera. Does seeing the reader help you sense the mood, or does the picture of the reader provide a distraction? Familiarity with all kinds of music is one of the most sought-after qualifications for both radio and television personnel. Records of "mood music" are available and are most helpful, but such records cannot provide the enormous variety needed as background for a wide range of programs.

THE SECRET LIFE OF ANDREW TARDY

by Beverly Manney*

(with apologies to James Thurber)

MUSICAL INTRODUCTION (CRESCENDO OF 10 SEC.)

ANNOUNCER (SLOW, BOOMING VOICE):	WMHS presents - The Secret Life of Andrew Tardy!!
MUSIC: DIMINUENDO OF 10 SEC.	
Narrator (more intimate):	The story of Andy Tardy is the story of any high school youth. He is the typical teen-age hero, not a bit like the ones familiar to radio listeners and movie fans. He didn't get the starring role in the school play; in fact, he didn't get any role at all. He didn't make the eighty yard run to beat New Rochelle in the last minutes of the game because he was only a substitute for the third team. He isn't editor of the paper or president of the G.A. Andy didn't win the public speaking contest - he didn't even compete. He was too scared. He enjoys the famous little pleasures of youth - like the ecstatic thrill of having his own car, even if his father only let him keep it three days. He looks forward to the luxury of a study hall nap mostly to avoid suspicion of being an eager beaver - a conscientious student. And he enjoys an illegitimate cigarette - even though he coughs on it. He is careful to ask for a ''Coke'' - never a

*Written while a student in a radio production class at Mamaroneck Senior High School, Mamaroneck, New York.

Coca-cola. You wouldn't think it, but he
notices every girl that passes. He won't say
so, but he likes the clink of her jewelry,
and the sloppy shoes she wears. He knows she
is an affected actress in everything she
does. But he likes it. Few people understand
him - because he changes so much from one
stage to the other. But most of all he's a
dreamer. He dreams fantastic dreams and
knows they won't come true. But sometime
he'll dream a dream he wants to live. Then he
will no longer be a complex embryo of a
future world - he will be a citizen of today.
Occasionally, Andy has a date - even if he
has to call up three different girls. He
takes the train to the movies - seldom goes
to a dance. We meet our hero on his way to
New Rochelle with Mary Robertsox, who is his
date. She is a pretty girl and Andy is glad
to see that people are noticing them. . . .
By the way, we want to add that any
similarity between characters in the
program and those in the audience is purely
intentional. The couple is walking along
Main Street, and Mary suddenly exclaims:

MARY:	Oh, look at the cute guys in uniform!
ANDY:	Yeah.
MARY:	Gee, did you see the ribbons the tall one had!
ANDY:	Yeah.

DREAM MUSIC: 10 SEC. - FADE OUT

COLONEL: Well, men, I guess we're finished. That tank
ahead is coming this way. You have all been
good soldiers. Let us die like men.

ANDY:	Wait, Colonel. I have a plan. Give me a grenade! I'm going out to get that tank.
COLONEL:	Why, Tardy, that's sheer suicide. You'll never make it. They'll cut you to ribbons.
ANDY:	Cigarette, Colonel?
COLONEL:	Here, have a shot of brandy, old man.
ANDY:	Thanks.
COLONEL:	Man, you can hold that liquor. Before you go, my boy, I want you to know that if we get out of here alive, I'm recommending you for a decoration. May I - shake your hand?
ANDY:	So long.
COLONEL:	Bless you, my boy. (COMMAND - LOUD) Company attention! Present arms to a brave man - Private Andrew Tardy!

DREAM MUSIC: UP FULL 10 SEC. - OUT WITH STINGER

MARY:	Andy, what's the matter with you? You almost got hit by that car.
ANDY:	I was just thinkin'.
MARY:	What about?
ANDY:	Oh, nothin'.
MARY:	Well, what movie do you want to see?
ANDY:	I don't care. Which one would you like?
MARY: (OVERDRAMATIC)	Well, Andy, I feel romantic tonight. I feel it deep inside me, like the music of an orchestra in my heart. Let's go see Humphrey Bogart.
ANDY:	Okay.
NARRATOR:	And so Andy and Mary went into the theater, went upstairs and began to squeeze in front of all the people's knees, and finally dropped into their seats. For a few moments they sat there watching the colorful travelogue scenery of a Mexican desert. In

	Andy's mind the question surged -
ANDY:	Should I hold her hand? Should I hold her hand?
NARRATOR:	Andy lit a cigarette, just like Paul Newman. He slid his arm to the armrest and like a stealthy panther's leap he suddenly gripped her hand.
MARY: (VERY MUCH ALOUD)	Oh look, there's Bill! Hi, Bill!
ANDY: (VERY MUCH SUBDUED)	'Lo, Bill.
MARY:	Oh, wasn't he swell in the Bellows game?
ANDY:	Yup.

DREAM MUSIC: UP FULL 10 SEC. - HOLD UNDER

BOY'S VOICE:	Well, fellows, I guess we're licked. We only need one touchdown to win, and here we are on our own forty yard line. Time for only one play.
ANDY:	Let me take the ball.
BOY:	You, Tardy???
ANDY:	I can try.
BOY:	What do we have to lose? Okay, Andy.
SPORTS ANNOUNCER:	Mamaroneck has the ball for the last play, folks. It looks like a New Rochelle three point victory. Well, it's Tardy back this time - standing calmly with his hands on his hips. The ball is snapped. Tardy races into the center of the line. He's down - NO! He's broken through like a steam engine, and he's in the clear. But wait, there's one more New Rochelle man. He's diving for Tardy's knees, but Tardy jumps high in the air to hurtle over the tackler! He's racing towards the goal line and the crowds are delirious. He's over! The crowds have surged onto the field

| | to hoist him on their backs. The mob is |
| | cheering Tardy!! |

DREAM MUSIC: OUT WITH STINGER

MARY:	What a kiss! Oh, he's my man.
ANDY:	Whattzat?
MARY:	Weren't you watching? Bogey just kissed
	Lauren.
ANDY:	Oh.

DREAM MUSIC: UP 10 SEC. - HOLD UNDER

SULTRY WOMAN:	Got a match, Andy?
ANDY:	Whaddya wanna do, start a flame in my heart?
WOMAN:	Say, I could go for you in a big way.
ANDY:	Listen, sister, I know you dames like a
	book. Here, have a drink. I always take mine
	straight. Yeah, I've known 'em like you.
	Beautiful but dangerous. I've been around.
	Paris, Trinidad, Hong Kong - everywhere. The
	world's my home, see? So I'm no good for any
	woman. . . . . Don't get so close
	to me.
WOMAN:	You don't like me?
ANDY:	It's that perfume.
WOMAN:	Don't hold me so tight.
ANDY:	I love you, you little fox - I love you!
MARY:	Andy, don't squeeze my hand like that. Do
	you want to break it?
ANDY:	Yes, you little fox, I love you!
MARY:	You what???
ANDY:	Oh, I didn't . . . . .
MARY:	Andy Tardy, what's the matter with you?
ANDY:	Look, on the screen. There's the President.
MARY:	Yes, he's with the Secretary of State. Gosh,
	it must be wonderful to be famous like that
	and do big, important things.

DREAM MUSIC: UP FULL, FADE AND HOLD UNDER

NEWS COMMENTATOR: This is Wallace Klondike, speaking to you
                                     from Washington. This is certainly a
                                     magnificent scene before me, ladies and
                                     gentlemen. I am standing before the Capitol
                                     and as far as I can see crowds of people are
                                     assembled to witness this momentous
                                     occasion. Tardy the genius is due to arrive
                                     at any moment. Dozens of searchlights
                                     illuminate the whole district with the light
                                     of day. Airplanes and helicopters hover
                                     constantly overhead. The crowd is restless,
                                     and I can hear the shuffling of thousands of
                                     feet. The entire police force is on duty
                                     this evening and traffic is at a standstill
                                     as thousands await the arrival of Tardy's
                                     motorcade from the airport.

SOUND: SHOUTS, POLICE SIRENS, MORE SHOUTS

NEWS COMMENTATOR: Here he is now, folks, arriving at the
                                     Capitol steps. He's being led by military
                                     escort to the microphone. All America is
                                     waiting to hear what this world famous
                                     figure has to say.

SOUND: SHOUTS, CROWD NOISES

NEWS COMMENTATOR: Flash bulbs are going off in every direction
                                     as news photographers vie with each other to
                                     get a picture of the one and only Andrew
                                     Tardy.

DREAM MUSIC: UP AND OUT WITH STINGER

MARY: Andy, what's the matter with you? The
                                     movie's over. Let's get out of here while
                                     the lights are on.

ANDY: What's that . . . . . . er, oh, yes . . . .
                                     excuse us, please. I'm sorry, Mary, I guess

NARRATOR: I was thinking about something else.
And so our hero and his friend leave the theater and saunter along the street toward Mary's house. At the door Mary pauses with anticipation.

MARY: Thanks, Andy, for taking me to the movies.

ANDY: Yeah, that's all right. I enjoyed it too.
Well, I guess I'll see you in school.
G'night.

MARY: Andy - aren't you going to kiss me?

ANDY: Me?

MARY: Then I'll kiss you. . . . . G'night, Andy.

ANDY: Gee. . . . . . G'night.

NARRATOR: And so the typical high school boy turns dreamily from the porch. He walks lightly - almost on his toes. His eyes shine and his lips have a crooked, vivid red smile.

MUSIC: CRESCENDO FOR 10 SEC. FADE UNDER AND OUT

ANNOUNCER: You have been listening to the Radio Workshop Players in ''The Secret Life of Andrew Tardy,'' an original script by Beverly Manney. Appearing in today's cast were:

    Bill Robinson as Andy

    Dale Dacier as Mary

    Tenny Schad as the Colonel

    Paul Field as the football player

    Bernie Titlebaum as the sports announcer

    Beverly Mitten as the woman

    Bill Burns as the news commentator.

Don Breen and Dave Hall were in charge of production. Bill Willkinson has been your announcer.

Additional Resources

Buxton, Frank and Bill Owen. *Radio's Golden Age*. New York: Easton Valley Press, 1966.

Rhymer, Frances, ed. *The Small House Halfway Up in the Next Block*. New York: McGraw-Hill, 1972. Thirty scripts from the old radio show, *Vic and Sade*.

Lass, A. H., Earle McGill, and Donald Axelrod, eds. *Plays from Radio*. Boston: Houghton-Mifflin, 1948.

Cassettes:

Center for Cassette Studies, Inc.
8110 Webb Avenue
North Hollywood, Calif. 91605

Records:

"Golden Memories of Radio"

"I Remember Radio"

Longines Symphonette Society
Longines Square
Larchmont, N.Y. 10538

Audio Tapes:

Mr. Charles Schoden
Station WLTD
2100 Lee Street
Evanston, Ill. 60202

Mar Bren Sound Company
420 Pelham Road
Rochester, N.Y. 14610

National Center for Audio Tapes
Stadium Building
University of Colorado
Boulder, Col. 80302

Radio Yesteryear
Box H
Croton-on-Hudson, N.Y. 10520

5

Transmitting the Message

Before the engineers and technical staff electronically transmit your message over the airwaves or over the coaxial cable, (a cable for sending telephone, telegraph, and television impulses consisting of an insulated conductor tube surrounding a central core of conducting material), there is another kind of "transmission" with which you must be concerned in order to prevent interference in the communication process. Literally, *transmit* means to "send across." In the television studio, the message must be "transmitted," or "sent across," to the camera and microphone with faithful adherence to the intent of the communicator and with consideration for the receiver of the message in front of a television set. Nothing that happens or fails to happen in the studio process must be allowed to distract the viewer from the objective the communicator has in mind.

For instance, if you are transmitting a commercial for a product and your eyes obviously wander to the floor manager's hand signals, the viewer's attention is drawn to your awkward eye movements rather than to the desirable traits of the product you are promoting. Suppose you are presenting an interview with an outstanding science student, and your words are blurred because you do not use the microphone correctly. The people listening to you in front of the television set have to concentrate so intently on hearing the actual words that they cannot focus on the meaning of what you are saying. Suppose your theater group is televising a scene in a mood of sorrow and deep grief. The viewer responds with hilarity rather than sympathy because the shadow of the boom mike creates the effect of a telephone pole emerging from the head of one of the tragic characters.

The Production Team

Effectively transmitting the message from the communicator in the studio to the television viewer is a team responsibility. It involves the technicians, who keep the equipment operating effi-

Transmitting messages to the television viewer is a team responsibility. Equally important is that talent understand what each member of the studio crew is doing or failing to do.

ciently; the director, who orchestrates the human and technical elements into a harmonious whole; the studio crew, who operate the equipment in the studio; the floor manager, who relays the director's instructions to the talent (performers); the talent, or performer, who is transmitting an idea, a musical selection, a dance, or a magic act to a camera and microphone. Any member of this team can create the kind of distraction or interference that prevents the message from getting across to the viewer.

You may never function as a floor manager, a camera operator, or a boom operator, but as the talent on a program you need to know what each of them can do to and for you as he or she performs or fails to perform his or her job on the studio crew.

Floor Managers

Floor managers cue the talent when it's time to begin. They give the time cues when there is one minute left, when the talent must

The floor manager is the director's representative in the studio. That person actually runs the show in the studio and must operate in complete silence.

conclude or wind up his or her part of the program, and when he or she must stop. They are responsible for relaying the director's instructions, which are received via a headset, to those in the studio who are not wearing headsets. They may help the talent by lifting the mike cable to keep them from tripping over it, or by signaling a graphics assistant to flip over the cards on which photographs are mounted. They will cue the talent when to look toward another camera, when to speak louder, and when to cross to a different position.

The floor manager must avoid getting in front of the camera; he or she must be the director's representative in the studio, actually running the show in the studio. All this must be done silently, in pantomime, with hand signals that you should learn so they can help you perform your job correctly.

Camera Operators

Camera operators are obviously vital members of the studio team. The extent to which they can make or break your performance is suggested by the insistence of some movie personalities that only their personally selected camera operators be allowed to

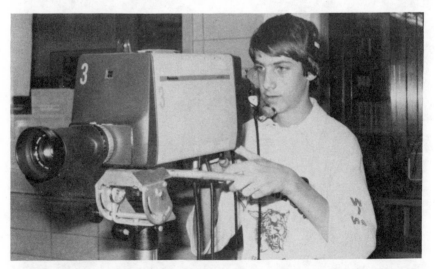

In many schools, camera operators work with talent and the floor manager during rehearsals, then operate on their own—with no director during production. In effect, they function as their own director.

shoot scenes in which they appear. A camera operator can shoot you at a most uncomplimentary angle, adding pounds to your weight, inches to your nose, and shadows to your eyes.

Camera techniques can assist the director in establishing a viewpoint for the listener at home. In *The Selling of the President, 1968*, author Joe McGinniss reported that one of Richard Nixon's television advisers, William Gavin, recommended that in televising a speech made by the President, the camera sweep over the audience. This would show the home viewers what President Nixon saw, put them in Nixon's position and show what he was up against. The camera would make the viewers partners with Nixon, looking through the same eyes.

In many schools and small studios camera operators may serve on different occasions as directors, audio persons, floor managers, or as performers when they are not behind their cameras. They may work with a director who gives precise instructions as to their every move, or they may have a director who gives few instructions, depending upon them to follow a shot sheet and frame pictures ready for use. A common arrangement in school studios is to have the operator of a single camera work with the talent and the floor manager during rehearsal, then work on his or her own, with no director, during production. In that way, the camera operator is actually functioning as his or her own director.

Rehearsal procedure.   If you function in a setup where you operate a camera, you will need to check the following procedures:

1. Put on a headset, if there is one, to receive instructions from the control room.
2. Uncap the lens and place the cap where you can find it at the end of the program. Don't carry it home in your pocket by mistake!
3. Determine what f stop you will set the lens aperature to. Most studios use f 5.6 for greatest depth of field. Remember that if you want less, open the f stop; if you want more, close the f stop. When you are finished, be sure to close the lens.
4. If your camera has a viewfinder, check to see if reflecting lights interfere with the picture. If there is no hood to shade the viewfinder, you may want to tape on a cardboard reflector to shade the viewfinder from the glare of lights.

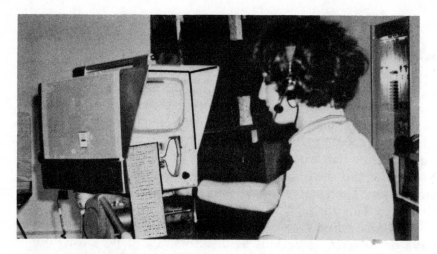

A shot sheet lists in order the shots a camera is to take. This sheet is taped to the back of the camera near the viewfinder. It is usually four inches wide and twelve inches long.

5. Check cable and AC power lines to be sure that power is coming to the camera and that a picture can be transmitted from the camera.
6. Unlock the panning head, and try panning left and right and tilting up and down.
7. Truck and dolly across the studio floor to be sure you can move the camera quickly and surely on command.
8. Check the focus by shooting a test-pattern card if you have one; then focus on various areas of the studio to make certain you can get a clear picture of each area.
9. Check the focus also by shooting at a variety of visuals, graphics, and set props.
10. If you are going to use a shot sheet, check every shot you can frame up in advance to be sure you can give the director and/or talent the picture requested.

Shot sheet: camera # 1

1. Wide shot of classroom
2. Two-shot of teacher and Bill
3. HS shot of Bill
4. CU of key in Bill's hand
5. Two-shot of teacher and Bill
6. HS shot of teacher
7. CU of teacher
8. Wide shot of classroom

ETV - CCTV - VTR STANDARD TEST PATTERN

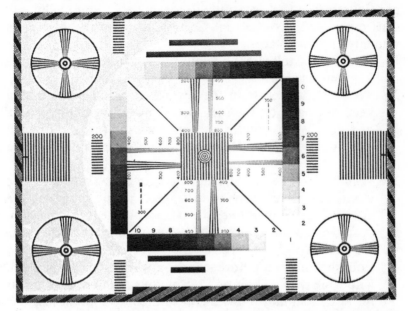

11. During rehearsals, ask questions whenever you are not sure what is wanted, since you will not be able to talk during the actual production. Even though you have intercom equipment, the sound of your voice will be picked up by a studio mike. If the director asks you questions, he or she will be careful to phrase them so they can be answered by *yes* or *no*, and you will have been instructed to blow into the mike once for *yes* and twice for *no*.

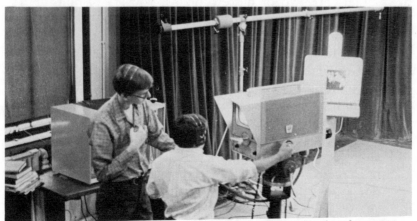

Obviously, a camera operator cannot speak during the actual performance. So be sure all questions are asked during rehearsals.

Production procedure. During the actual production, your procedure will differ according to the control room facilities and staff available in your setup. Certain procedures, however, are standard in most places.

1. Wait for the tally light on your camera to go out before moving your camera.

2. To keep the picture in focus while your camera is moving, keep one hand on the focus knob when you dolly, pan, tilt, or truck. When you dolly back, turn the focus knob clockwise; when you dolly forward, turn the focus counterclockwise.

3. Watch the mike and the camera cables on the studio floor. Don't dolly over them or disconnect them by kicking them out of place. Some camera operators place the cables on their shoulders so the cables will be out of the way as they move the camera.

4. Look behind you before a fast outward or backward dolly. Knocking over a chair or a set of gongs can create a distracting noise that may motivate the director to commit justifiable homicide.

5. It is wise to be aware (in the periphery of your vision) of any of the performer's movements that suggest he or she is going to stand, lift a visual, or walk to the side. However, you should concentrate on the viewfinder of your camera, constantly aware that the picture you frame in that viewfinder will be the one that communicates meaning to the television viewer.

6. If there are two or more cameras, you are responsible for keeping out of range of these other cameras.

7. If the director permits you to frame shots and select shooting angles, remember that (a) pointing the camera upward from a lower angle gives dominance and power to the performer; (b) pointing the camera downward on the performer gives him or her the appearance of weakness and inferiority; (c) an extreme wide-angle lens can distort close-ups for comic or grotesque effect; (d) an extreme wide-angle lens can give apparent depth to a room, or length to an object angled toward the camera. Notice how the dramatic effect of close-ups is used more often in soap operas than in television newscasts.

8. Any decision you make on your own should fit in with the mood and purpose of the show. A tight close-up of a fly on

the end of the teacher's twitching nose may be an entertaining reaction shot, but it will be poor television if the aim of the program is to explain how to use the shift key on the typewriter.

Striking the set.   At the end of the show during which you have served as camera operator, close the f stop, replace the cap on the lens, coil the cable, and fasten it neatly. Lock the panning head. Dolly the camera to the side of the studio near a wall. Lock the wheels of the dolly. Assist other members of the student crew in striking or dismantling the set; return all pieces of equipment to their storage location, return all borrowed set props, and see that the studio is in order.

ECONOMY NOTE. The cardboard cylinders from toilet tissue and paper-towel rolls make excellent, inexpensive containers to hold 12″ loops of cable for storage.

Audio Technicians

Another crew member of this studio team is the audio technician. Like the camera operator and the floor manager, the technician's duties and responsibilities vary greatly according to the facilities

The person handling audio controls exercises aesthetic judgment, listens to sound as an interpretation of mood, and is sensitive to the subtle effects of tone quality.

and staff available. In some studios you, the performer, will plug in your own mike and place the lavaliere cord around your neck; in others you will not touch the mike or any of the audio controls.

In general, however, audio technicians are responsible for the sounds from the mikes and for electronically produced sounds played in the control room or studio. Good audio technicians do more than turn mikes on and off, and volume up and down. They exercise aesthetic judgment, listen to sounds as interpretations of mood, and are sensitive to the subtle effects of tone quality. If you are given the assignment of audio technician, these are some of the duties you will be expected to perform:

1. Check with the director and/or performer to find out what records, tapes, carts, and cassettes will be needed. Check cues, mark the script, and mark the records and tapes. Check equipment to be sure you know how to operate it at the correct speed, on cue, with all feed lines connected and functioning.

2. Check with the director and/or performer as to what kinds of mikes are needed, where they must be located, and whether they are to be on (live) all the time or on and off according to cue.

3. Connect mikes and check cables to see that they are out of the way and out of sight if possible.

4. During rehearsals, see that all performers use the mikes properly. Be sure to make this check while they are standing or moving exactly as they will be during production.

5. Write down where each mike is located on the control board. Don't risk turning up two or three pots (volume control dials on the audio board, usually calibrated from 0 to 100) during the show before the announcer's mike finally comes on.

6. "Get a level" on each performer; that is, determine the volume of his or her voice and the corresponding volume at each mike. Write it down: "Mrs. Mendez, 80–90. Flutist at mike 2, 70–100. John, 75–80." The volume will vary during the performance, but these figures will give you an approximate idea of the range to be expected from each speaker or performer. If you operate the controls during the performance, you will have to "ride gain" (keeping the hand on audio controls and watching the needle that registers the

amount of volume being fed through audio lines) throughout the show, ready to anticipate action. After a performer
shouts into the mike, it is too late to turn down the volume,
since the next words may be spoken very softly.

7. If a lavaliere mike is to be used, be sure the cord is adjusted
to avoid entanglement with beards, long hair, ties, or
jewelry.

8. If the boom mike is used, be sure the operator knows when
and where he or she can and must move. Check the shadows
cast by the boom to be sure they are not visible on walls
where camera operators will be framing pictures.

9. After the show, disconnect the mikes and return them to
their storage area with cables coiled and fastened. If a portable amplifier has been used, it should be disconnected and
stored.

10. Assist other crew members in striking the set and returning
the studio to order.

Production Assistants

An important part of the studio team is the personnel responsible
for the placement and manipulation of graphics and props. These
production assistants may also help prepare the props and construct suitable stands on which to display visuals for good camera
pick-up.

Their task may be to construct an easel-like stand with an extension at eye level for holding graphics. This "hod" as it is
sometimes called, may have the metal spine of a three-ring
looseleaf notebook nailed to the top of the hod so that graphic
cards with three holes punched in the top can be flipped up or
down into camera range. The shelf may have ridges or tracks to
enable production assistants to slide graphic cards horizontally
into camera range.

Another necessary job may be to see that the dark-colored
lay-ons to be placed on the pastel-colored flannel board all have
sandpaper backing securely glued in place to help them adhere to
the flannelboard. A production assistant may also be assigned to
provide an adequate supply of dry ice to simulate steam, or to
number all the graphics on the back in the order in which they
will be displayed on camera. Sometimes, menu board like that

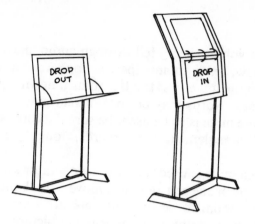

An example of a "hod" (right) in which the spine of a loose-leaf binder is used and a special stand (left) used so that graphic cards can be flipped up or down into camera range.

used in cafeterias showing the entres with plastic letters is useful. These letters can be inserted easily, and a shot of the board for graphics can be used. It makes an excellent super or key with a person's name.

ECONOMY NOTE: The rough-textured paper in a wallpaper sample book makes an excellent background for graphics. Stores will give you old sample books free.

A studio prop that production assistants can construct sounds more exciting than it is, e.g., the strip tease, used for revealing words or numerals one at a time. Words, phrases, or statistics are covered with strips of paper or cardboard, which can be removed one by one to reveal the hidden words or data on cue. Plastic tape on the back of a line graph can be removed an inch at a time, letting the light shine through and giving the effect of a moving graph line.

Properties.   If you are a production assistant, one of the most interesting challenges to your ingenuity will be the creation of props that will look real on camera. For example, you will probably need to make "synthetic blood," an essential ingredient in so many commercial television programs nowadays, with violence portrayed in living color. Catsup can be used for blood on the stage, and black-and-white films have found chocolate syrup satisfactory; but color television has required the development of "technicolor blood" and "panchromatic blood." It is possible to purchase a pint of synthetic blood that consists of microscopic red plastic balls suspended in a liquid and can be thickened or thinned to the desired consistency.

Truth in advertising.   The production assistant's job has been further complicated by a regulation intended to protect the consumer from fraudulent claims for products, the FCC ruling that only real products can be shown in television commercials. Artificial coloring or synthetic devices cannot be substituted for products on camera. Because human vision and camera vision do not perceive objects and colors in the same way, production assistants would often add grenadine to orange juice to keep it from looking like milk; add shoe polish to coffee to give it that "rich, full-bodied look"; and tint spaghetti with yellow food coloring. The truth-in-advertising regulation makes it necessary for a commercial television studio to photograph the real item. Fortunately, this does not apply to a school production, which remains strictly a closed-circuit operation.

An ice cream commercial requires gallons of the product, as the melted cream must be replaced after each shot under the hot lights. Egg whites cannot be substituted for the beer "head," which also melts away under the heat of the lights. Filming a one-minute beer commercial may use up eight cases of beer. So the production assistant has to check each item on camera to determine in advance how to make real objects appear real—a most demanding and exacting assignment, requiring patience and ingenuity.

Technical Directors, Switchers

When they are functioning in the studio, the production assistants, audio technician, camera operator, and floor manager are all under the supervision of the director. In many studios, school and commercial, there is a technical director who operates the switches and buttons in the control room to effect the change from one camera to the other on command from the director: "Take 1. Dissolve to 2. Super 1. Go to black." However, passing a command from one person to another can affect the split-second timing needed in cutting from one camera to another. In many cases, therefore, the director must be, or prefers to be, his or her own technical director. Some studios do not use a technical

Often, where the director also serves as technical director, a "switcher" is used to immediately execute changes ordered by the director.

director. They have a switcher who actually pushes the buttons and immediately executes the changes from one camera to another as ordered by the director. Directors often use "*ready* to take one" or "*ready* to dissolve to two" to prepare the switcher for the next move.

Directors

In television, the relationships between directors and their teams, and the nature of their responsibilities, differ from those in both theater and radio. The stage director of a play has little, if any, control over the performers once they appear on the stage, but may cue lights, sound, and curtain from a position offstage. The radio director, on the other hand, is in constant communication with the cast through hand signals and cues. The television director has audio contact with the camera operators and floor manager, who is the director's only contact with the performers.

Television directors, then, have a special communication problem in achieving the effects they wish to create.

Advance preparation.   Because television directors must achieve a maximum of coordination in a minimum of allotted time, they must prepare carefully in advance. They may call on production assistants for many jobs—timing the script, taking notes at rehearsals, and running errands. Studio time is usually limited and expensive; so is the time of the engineers and technical personnel. Therefore directors try to make every minute in the studio count. They hold "dry runs"—that is, rehearsals without the cameras turned on. The director makes a floor plan, marking where each set piece will be, where talent will be, where cameras will be, where movements will extend. In short, any decisions that simplify and speed up the rehearsal should be made by the director before calling the performers to the studio.

Picture sequence.   To produce television pictures that will communicate a desired message, you as the director will have to plan successive camera shots to get that meaning across. You must think in terms of not only pictures but of the sequence in which the viewer must see those pictures. Suppose the program features a youth symphony orchestra. You will have to instruct camera #2 to frame and focus picture #2 (a close-up of the guest pianist), while camera #1 is taking picture #1 (a wide shot of the

SIMPLE FLOOR PLAN

For really effective rehearsals, a floor plan that indicates where each set piece will be, where talent will be located, where cameras will be, where movements will extend, etc. is essential.

entire orchestra). While the viewer is watching picture #2 (the guest pianist) being transmitted from camera #2, you must instruct camera #1 to frame and focus picture #3 (a shot of the violin section with the first violinist in the foreground). You must think ahead, keeping the viewer's needs in mind and remaining ever alert to the potentialities and limitations of the cameras you have available. To have the right shots readied and taken at the proper time, you will need skill that can be developed only with much practice. To coordinate what you are doing with what everyone else is doing requires visual imagination, efficiency, and advance planning. Even though you have created communicative pictures in your mind, the viewer will never see those pictures unless the engineer, the camera operators, and the talent know what you want and are placed in a position to transmit each picture at the time you call for it.

Pointers for the director.   Even in simple productions like class exercises, the director can profit by following these suggestions.

1. Rehearse with the performers outside the studio. Correct the way they say and do things before they face the cameras.
2. Work out all the camera positions, angles, and details ahead of time by using a floor plan. See that your cameras can get all the shots before you walk into the studio. It is expensive to keep a cast and crew waiting as you work out camera positions that could have been worked out ahead of time.
3. Write a shot sheet or cue sheet for each camera operator so he or she will know that the first shot will be a CU of the professor's glasses and the second shot an HS shot of the professor. Then, if you become too busy or too excited during the show to give each camera operator adequate advance directions to ready his or her shot, he or she will find them on the shot sheet.
4. Mark difficult-to-remember locations on the studio floor, using chalk or tape. If talent must stand in a certain spot to be properly lighted or to be within mike range, mark that spot on the floor.
5. Rehearse production assistants in the operation of flip cards, pictures on an easel, strip-tease tear-offs, and other properties to be manipulated on cue.

6. Check difficult shots, such as those of a typewriter keyboard reflected in an overhead mirror. The mirror should be angled and fastened in the best possible position for effective camera work *before* the cast and crew report for rehearsal. Don't keep twelve people waiting while you search for the correct length of pipe and the necessary screwdriver.

7. If you have two copies of a book or picture, one to be held by the talent and the other to be shot close-up in limbo (that is, with no specific background—against a curtain or blank wall), check the distance and size of these shots before the group arrives in the studio. You may want to have one camera operator arrive early to run through these difficult shots.

8. As you plan your shots, remember how small the viewing screen is. (A twenty-five-inch screen is considered large.) Bear in mind that close-ups and medium shots that fill most of the screen will be clearer than long shots of numerous small objects.

9. Make your instructions to the crew clear, concise, and definite. Use precise language such as, "Dolly in on the silver cup for a close-up in which we can read the inscription." Then the camera operators know what to do and how they can tell when they have the right shot.

10. Keep calm. Keep your mind on what you're doing. Control your temper.

11. Remember to keep a cover shot for yourself. A cover shot allows you to shoot the entire situation when you're not sure what is going to happen next. In a panel discussion, for example, if you are not sure who is going to talk next, get a shot of the entire group until you know.

12. Concentrate on producing a sound and picture sequence that will communicate the message to the television viewer with a single impact and hence without interference.

Any student who has experienced some of the trials and thrills of directing a television program will appreciate the truth behind the somewhat facetious suggestions in these "Ten Commandments of Television":

1. Thou shalt show the viewer what he wants to see when he wants to see it.

2. Thou shalt not show a person speaking about an object which is out of the camera's frame at the moment.
3. Thou shalt have the right person on the screen at the right time: the speaker when he speaketh, the reactor when he reacteth.
4. Thou shalt not cross thy cables, but thou shalt cross thy cameras, shooting across each other's angles, when thy subjects are of equal importance.
5. Thou shalt not reverse thy screen direction by showing the same person moving or looking L to R in one shot and R to L in the next.
6. Thou shalt not leave thy cameraman guessing as to what his next shot may be, but shall ready each camera as soon as it is off the air.
7. Thou shalt not forget that the TV screen is a small screen, and the close-up is the all-important shot.
8. Thou shalt not neglect an establishing shot, showing thy viewer the relation between this, that, and the other.
9. Thou shalt not cut from camera to camera for no good reason, or without motivation, or just to lend variety to thy shots.
10. Thou shalt not stay too long in black, lest they viewer kick his set reproachfully, thinking it hath conked out again.

by Rudy Bretz, and Edward Stasheff
from *The Television Program: Its Direction and Production*

The Talent's Responsibilities

No director is skillful enough to communicate a message clearly without the cooperation of the talent. If performers are ill at ease, if they do not use the mike properly, if they do not cooperate with the studio crew, if they are not alert to the director's instructions as relayed through the floor manager, if their message for the viewer is not clear in their minds, if they are not aware of the demands of the medium through which they are trying to reach the viewer—then they will be responsible for causing interference that will distract the viewer, and may in extreme cases obliterate the message from the consciousness of the viewer.

As a performer you have to know how to work with two kinds of production staffs; (1) student groups—most likely to staff your school production center, and (2) a professional studio production staff—with whom you will work if you are invited to appear on a local commercial or educational station program.

If you are an on-camera performer in a school studio with a classmate as director and an inexperienced camera operator, you will have to think of their problems as well as your own and anticipate what they will have to do. If you are an on-camera performer in a commercial studio, you will have to follow directions as you receive them and cooperate with the staff in carrying out instructions, some of which may be based on union regulations. A school in New York was fined $250 because, during a presentation in a commercial studio, a student moved a spotlight contrary to the stagehands' union rules.

As an on-camera performer you will need to put into practice every principle of effective speaking and communication that you have ever learned. Individuals who are successful in expressing themselves in their professions or their daily jobs sometimes get "mike fright" and "clam up" on television. Although the following tips were prepared by the Illinois State Medical Society for doctors participating in a televised program, they will be equally helpful to a student who is inexperienced in performing on camera.

1. Do not memorize the script. Conversation should be as flexible and casual as possible. The script is prepared for continuity and cut material, not for specific dialogue.

2. Do not remain too long with any one chart or other prop. This is tiring to the viewer. After one or two charts or diagrams have been used for about a minute, walk away, *slowly*, to another part of the set as outlined by the director. Then, when necessary, return to the chart for another brief discussion.

3. Equipment that calls for camera close-ups should be held quietly in the hands and horizontally in front of the body. This is particularly true of shiny objects because of reflection, and of diagrams because of blurred image. Better yet, hold objects and charts on a table so they will not move.

4. A rehearsal, without cameras, is called a dry-run. With cameras, it is called a camera rehearsal. Listen to the instructions given in the studio so that you will know which camera is focused on you without appearing that you are being given signals by the stage director.

5. Do not talk *up* to or *at* a boom mike. This mike is very sensitive. Talk naturally. If you are using a lavalier mike, don't play with the mike. Any movement will create noise that will be picked up. Don't talk into the lavalier mike. Talk over it as you look into the camera.

6. When patients are used, introduce them informally. They will not understand their cue for appearance, so call them by name to bring them on the set. Be natural and friendly. Dismiss them the same way with a word of thanks.

7. Do not indulge in long, detailed explanations. With a physician-moderator on the program, a flow and exchange of discussion is possible and important. The objective is to present one phase and not the entire subject in each program. Combine discussion with action.

8. When a medical term is used, explain it in lay language.

Facial expression. As an on-camera performer you—like the doctors for whom the medical association prepared the foregoing television tips—will need to remember that the most frequently used shots of you will probably be head and shoulders. Therefore, your facial expression will give the viewer clues as to your sincerity and general attitude. The expression in your eyes is the most revealing communicator you have. In your eyes, the viewer can read more than he or she can in your language. When you roll your eyes you tell the viewer, "I'm only kidding; this really isn't that important." A furtive glance to the side can say, "I'm more worried about that next timing cue than I am about the boat people from Viet Nam." Raising the eyebrows can criticize or condemn as caustically and bitterly as words.

Bowing your head over your notes leaves the camera operator with only the top of your head as a picture communicating your message. Licking your lips or covering part of your face with your hand draws attention to the mannerism and away from the message.

Facial expressions are important to the political campaigner who is trying to persuade his or her television audience. Former Vice-President Hubert Humphrey once said, "The biggest mistake in my political life was not to learn how to use television." The National Association of Broadcasters has prepared a booklet to assist candidates in using the intimate medium more effectively. Among its suggestions are these, which apply to anyone speaking on television:

1. Don't hold the script in front of your face. The audience expects to see *you* on television—not a piece of paper.

2. Action can be added by moving about—from the desk or table where you are seated to the charts, pictures, or

blackboard used to illustrate your message. But don't move about unnecessarily. It will only tend to distract the viewers.

3. Avoid meaningless gestures (such as twisting a pencil, which distracts the viewers) and sweeping gestures which may be lost to the camera's view.

4. Whether seated or standing, remember at all times to talk directly to the viewer. Keep in mind that the audience is *inside* the camera.

5. Keep always in mind that no matter how far from the camera you may be, it still is possible to take a close-up of your face. Since you have no way of knowing when a close-up is being made, act as if one is being taken at all times.

Since you have no way of knowing when a close-up is being made, act as if one is being taken at all times.

Bodily action.   Even though your director may concentrate on head and shoulder shots of you, your gestures and bodily actions are important. If you are sincerely concerned about what you are saying, your entire body will reflect that tension. So make no attempt to avoid gestures that express what you are feeling. Whether or not they show on camera, they will be evident in the tone of your voice. It is extremely difficult to project an alert, vital tone of voice from a slouchy, overly relaxed body frame.

Restricted movements.   During close-up shots you will need to keep your movements somewhat restricted to avoid going out of the picture frame on the left or on the right. Also, the close-up shots require you to keep gestures close to the body. If you extend them toward the camera, it will distort and magnify disproportionately those objects close to the lens.

Memory aids.   In most cases, the one thing the amateur on-camera performer fears above all is forgetting his or her lines. Whether the show is ad-lib (composed by the speaker impromptu) or scripted (everything from written script), you have a procedure to follow. If your mind "goes blank," you are embarrassed, and the viewer is equally uncomfortable. Even experienced professionals dread "blowing" lines and prepare all kinds of memory aids in advance.

Singers may have the lyrics written on large cue cards held near the camera lens. Teleprompters mounted on the camera carry the exact words of the script, printed in large letters on a television monitor located on top of the camera. A series of mirrors and one-way glass puts the script in front of the lens of the camera. In this way, the talent can look right into the lens as he or she reads the script. Unless the speaker and the operator of the teleprompter can rehearse together to establish the most desirable tempo, the speaker may have to speak faster than he or she wishes, or the operator may not be able to pace the roll of script to the speaker's varying tempo.

If you have watched telecasts of the political conventions, you might have glimpsed a one-way vision glass on which words were projected, visible to the speaker but not within range of the camera.

In a commercial, the script to be read may be attached to the back of a box of cereal or dog food as the product is held at eye level for the announcer. Books and similar stage props can hide a script on a desk or table.

David Frost, the talk-show host, did not try to hide the clip-board that held his notes for guest interviews. Johnny Carson often reads comments from the backs of pictures he is holding up for the camera. A minister was able to give "from memory" the full names of more than fifty babies he baptized on Easter Sunday by having their names typed on a card placed underneath the water in the baptismal font.

Performers in a dramatic show may look over the shoulders of other actors facing them and read their lines or cues on a teleprompter or cue card. Run-down lists or key phrases may be written on the studio floor. (Camera operators, beware of shooting low!) Newscasters often use both a script in hand and a teleprompting device. Viewers seem to feel that a report is more authentic and "documentary" if it comes from written copy.

Indeed, there are now so many variations of hidden and visible prompting devices that no on-camera performer need fear "going blank." Your only problem is how to read these prompting devices while still appearing to look directly into the camera. With experience, you can learn to look at your notes while the camera focuses on other participants. You will, however, give yourself away if you are caught glancing at your notes just as the camera returns to you.

Announcers

Announcers may read much of their material off camera in an "announce booth," or they may simply assume a position in which it is natural and acceptable to hold the script in front of them, with no attempt to disguise the fact that they are reading it.

As an announcer you should be especially mindful of the way you deliver your material. Your voice should be clear and pleasing, your articulation distinct, and your pronunciation flawless. In this list of commonly mispronounced words, the syndicated columnist Sydney Harris helps you to avoid some of the errors announcers often make.

A Primer for Announcers

Why don't pronouncing handbooks for radio and television announcers write it large and plain that:

—There is no "heal" in "helicopter," no "pear" in "irreparable," no "eggs" in "excerpts."

—There is no "z" in "absorbs," no "cull" in "culinary," and no "lug" in "luxury."

—There is no "may" in "menu," and no "ay" in "lingerie."

—There is no "peen" in "European," no "pie" in "impious," and no "zidge" in "exigency."

—The word "dour" is of Scottish origin, and rhymes with "moor," not with "our."

—A "glazier" is not an ice-formation, but a man who installs and repairs panes of glass.

—The opposite of "depth" is not "heighth," and the opposite of "weakness" is not "strenth."

—There is no such adjective as "preventative," and no such verb as "commentate"; medicine is "preventive," and commentators "comment."

—There is no "ouch" in "debauch," and no "vay" in "vagary."

—There is no "cue" in "coupon," no "pick" in "despicable," and, above all, no "spit" in "hospitable."

—There is no "dole" in "doldrums," no "he" in "heinous," and no "yum" in "columnist."

—There is no "pea" in "pianist," even when it's a concert pianist; there is no "zoo" in "zoology," and no "bert" in "sherbet."

—The "h" is not sounded in "La Boheme," the "g" is not sounded in "Pagliacci," and "Don Quixote" should not sound like a breakfast cereal.

—A "corespondent" in a divorce case is not pronounced the same as "correspondent" for a newspaper.

—There are three syllables, not two, in "finally"; three syllables, not four, in "parliament"; and five syllables, not four, in "incidentally."

—There is no "mere" in "premiere," no "mater" in "maitre d'hotel," and no "lounge" in a "chaise longue." There is no "home" in "homicide," no "hew" in "posthumous," and no "hose" in "hosiery."

—The finely expressive word "lambaste" rhymes with "paste" and not with "past."

SYDNEY J. HARRIS

If you are ad-libbing remarks to cover an emergency or to adjust to a changing situation, an occasional error in pronunciation might be excused, but it is unthinkable that you would mispronounce a proper name or a word in a script, which you have seen in advance of the performance. If you can't find the name of a composer or the title of a musical selection in your dictionary, ask one of the musicians, preferably the conductor. If you are not sure how to pronounce the name of guests you are interviewing, ask them, even if you have to do it at the beginning of the interview.

You cannot rely on rules for the pronunciation of geographical terms. If you mispronounce Des Plaines, Kanawha, Gallipolis, Willamette, Cairo, Terre Haute, Worcester, or Reading, the people who live there will not excuse or forgive your ignorance.

Ask an authority in your school about anglicizing words from other languages. Be consistent in using the native or the Americanized pronunciation of *chic, Goethe, alumnae, Michelangelo, fiance.* Check your dictionary for the correct pronunciation of these everyday words: *penalize, athletics, precedence, address, status, amateur, finance, adult, data.* Errors in pronunciation will distract the television viewer's attention away from your message and cast doubt upon your authority as a speaker in whom one should have confidence.

In summary, there are all manner of pitfalls that you, as a television communicator, must avoid as you transmit your message through the camera to people seated in front of their television sets. The more completely you can master production techniques, the more completely you can eliminate interference between yourself and the receiver of your message.

1. Discuss what general qualities any team should have to function effectively. Consider such elements as cooperation, communication, attitudes, and goals.

2. Consider the various duties and responsibilities discussed for each of the positions described. Does any position appeal to you more than another? Why? Why is it important to be aware of all the duties involved?

VIDEOLAB

1. Diagram a studio setup for a piano concert, with two cameras.

   Vary the width of the dotted-line triangles to indicate how much of the scene will be picked up by the camera; that is, just the keyboard or a long shot through the raised lid of the piano.

   After placing your figures on this floor plan of a studio, try these shots in your studio. Relocate the cameras if necessary to get the pictures you want. Then add to your diagram the placement of the mikes; M =floor mike, and BM

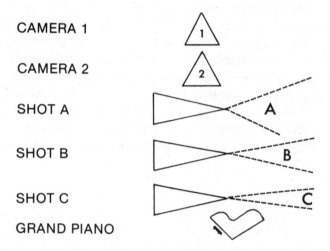

2. Make three copies of the following floor plan for an interview show.

   Using two cameras and moving the table and chairs any way you desire, diagram the location of cameras and types of camera shot (HS = head and shoulders, LS = long shot, CU = face of one person, 2-shot = both persons) you would use for each of these:

   a. The opening shot of the show to "establish" where the speakers are and how many there are.

   b. A shot during the guest's description of his or her early career.

c. The shot during the interviewer's closing remarks as he or she thanks the guest for participating in the program.

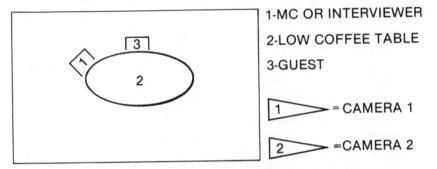

1-MC OR INTERVIEWER

2-LOW COFFEE TABLE

3-GUEST

1 ⊳ = CAMERA 1

2 ⊳ =CAMERA 2

3. Ask five of your classmates to prepare an original commercial for a product that can be brought into your classroom studio and promoted for sale. The six of you should draw a number from 1 to 6 and then rotate the crew assignments as indicated on the following chart. For instance, if you draw #3, you will operate camera 2 as student #1 presents the commercial; you will operate the mike as student #6 presents the commercial; you will direct student #5 as he or she presents the commercial; you will serve as a switcher as student #4 presents the commercial; during the fifth round you as student #3 will present your commercial; during the final round you will operate camera 1 as student #2 does the commercial.

	Talent	Camera 1	Camera 2	Audio	Director	Switcher
Round 1	Student #1	Student #2	Student #3	Student #4	Student #5	Student #6
Round 2	#6	#1	#2	#3	#4	#5
Round 3	#5	#6	#1	#2	#3	#4
Round 4	#4	#5	#6	#1	#2	#3
Round 5	#3	#4	#5	#6	#1	#2
Round 6	#2	#3	#4	#5	#6	#1

The length of each commercial should be determined by the length of your class period or television lab period. Each two-minute commercial will take a minimum of six or seven minutes to run through once in a rehearsal and then actually present it in a timed situation.

4. Rotate through these positions in a newsbreak assignment. Most television stations use a newsbreak or local news headlines during station breaks to keep viewers tuned to the later news. Plans to include a booth announcer, who will introduce the newsbreak with, "This is Channel 3 Newsbreak with _____. The anchorperson will appear on camera with two brief stories. You should have a script and a picture for each story mounted on tagboard. As the anchorperson reads the story, the picture will be shown on a camera. Go back to the anchorperson for the introduction of the second story, then go to the second picture. Go back to the anchorperson for the conclusion. At the end, the booth announcer says, "This is Channel 3 Newsbreak." The details to these and other stories can be seen on our ten (eleven) o'clock news." Perhaps you can use a key or super over the cover shot with the word "Newsbreak." Put this on the lower portion of the screen.

5. If there is a school or college near yours that also has a television studio, ask for permission to visit its control room during a rehearsal and broadcast. Take your cassette recorder with you and tape the director's instructions as he or she commands the camera operators, floor manager, and switcher, if one is used. Play the tape back several times to determine how clear the instructions were.

   If you have the opportunity to observe the control room of a commercial station, follow the same procedure. It will be especially helpful if you can be there during a station break between programs when there are several split-second actions to be timed. Tape the "patter" of the director for later study if you wish to try your hand at directing.

6. Invite a singer or guitarist to perform in your studio. First, listen to the song. Then decide what camera shots would show each idea used in the lines of the song. Determine whether to cut or dissolve when picture statements are to change. Video tape the performance and see if your pictures helped to reinforce ideas in the performance. Also, view directors as they televise singers. Watch the *Tonight Show* on NBC and see how the director helps the performers.

6

Verbalizing the Message

"I don't want a script. I want to sound natural. If I have a script, I'll sound stuffy. Besides—I can't memorize well; I'm afraid I'll forget." Does this sound familiar?

And haven't you also heard a student camera operator inquire plaintively, "When do you want the close-up of the transistor? How am I going to know when to dolly in on the table? How long do you expect me to stay with the tight shot on that transistor?"

Is a script necessary? It's obvious that a sportscaster can't prepare in advance a total script for the play-by-play account of a basketball game. On the other hand, a stand-up comedian can use memorized material, or a cue sheet, for opening jokes. Bob Hope, for instance, needs a large staff of writers who keep his material topical and appropriate to the locale and situation where he is performing. Does an M.C. need a script for interviews with the guests introduced on that show? Is the extempore (or unmemorized) style or ad-libbing more suitable for a comedian, and a scripted, memorized style more suitable for an actor or serious performer? Can you communicate better with or without a script? Why have a script at all?

Why Scripts Are Needed

Actors must obviously follow the script of the drama they are portraying. If they come to television from live theater, they are accustomed to giving exact word cues to other performers, and, therefore to following a script verbatim. In the interests of national security, federal officials often use prepared scripts to ensure the accuracy and correct documentation of everything they say. There are, however, three additional reasons for having a script, and these are important not only for the professional performer but also for the student working in a laboratory studio of a television production course.

1. To provide a smooth, attention-getting beginning and an effective wrap-up or conclusion.
2. To facilitate accurate, precise timing.
3. To provide the technical staff with the information necessary for them to supply the right pictures and sound at the right time.

Introduction and conclusion. For instance, the most awkward introduction an inexperienced, scriptless performer can use is simply, "Uh-h-h!" Another uninteresting ad-lib beginning is the dull "Well-uh, I'd like to start with. . . ." Scriptless conclusions can be equally ineffective, such as "Well, I guess that's about all."

Timing. For experienced professional performers, timing is less of a problem than it is for you. They know how much they can say in 30 seconds. They sense how fast they must talk to maintain a rate of 150 words a minute. They know about how long it takes to relate a certain anecdote and can add or subtract a minute by regulating the amount of detail they give. Yet you, who are learning to judge timing, may find yourself concluding lamely, "As I said before . . . ," or "And so, let me say again. . . ." "Egg on the face" describes your pained facial expression as you stare helplessly into a camera still focused on you when you have one minute of time left and nothing left to say.

Equally disconcerting is the plight of the inexperienced demonstrator who sees the final wrap-up time cue just as he or she comes to the most important step in assembling a model helicopter. You've probably heard an M.C. thanking guests in a rush, with an apologetic "We're a little late tonight, folks." The hurried remarks are followed by a full 60-second commercial, time that you probably feel could have been shared with the M.C. However, for every word of a commercial that is paid for but not used, the network must give a cash refund to the sponsor on a prorated basis. Money talks; therefore the M.C. must not!

Because of the importance of precise timing in television, you will need to have your script provide *if-cuts* and *cushions*. An "if-cut" is a part of the script that you can omit when time is running out. For example, suppose your script includes five examples of successful community programs for pollution control. The entire fourth example has been bracketed in the margin of the script and marked "if-cut." If the floor manager signals you to speed up, you can omit example four and proceed to example five, the most impressive of all. A "cushion" is material that can be used to stretch a program that is too short. It may be words, or music, or a sound effect. It may consist of alternative conclusions, varying in length, the appropriate one to be selected according to the time cues. Obviously, if-cuts and cushions are extremely difficult to handle without a script.

A guide for the crew.   To an even greater extent, the script is a lifesaver for the technical staff. If you've ever taken a long auto trip through new territory, you know how much help a road map can provide. If you've ever tried to assemble a child's toy without printed directions, you know the frustration of wondering which end you fold in first and how far the rod extends. The director and camera operators need the same kind of help in moving the mikes and the camera. After you've directed an ad-lib show, you'll appreciate even more the road map and directions a script provides.

There are experienced, skillful directors who can "wing it" or "fly by the seat of their pants," as they say. They have learned to make split-second decisions, to judge precisely what a camera operator can do, to estimate accurately the amount of picture that any size lens can shoot and to keep three shots ahead of the action. They cannot tell you how they do it any more than good pizza-makers can tell you how they know when they've put in enough oregano.

Completely Scripted Shows

Some types of show always require a complete script, such as the following:

1. *Plays*, which demand close-ups of actors' faces, business and movement essential to the plot, and reaction shots of one performer while the mike picks up the lines of another performer.
2. *Political talks*, in which critical, controversial issues must be discussed in exact terminology and carefully chosen phrases.
3. *Commercials*, in which claims for the product must use the limited time as effectively as possible.
4. *Reviews of sports*, in which accuracy of scores, players' names, and important features of many sports events must be crowded into a very brief time.
5. *News*, in which events must be reported in sequence to correlate with pictures, and in language that lends authenticity to the presentation.

Partially Scripted Shows

In partially scripted shows, such as the following, the introduction and conclusion have been prepared and certain transitions written into a script, but large portions are left to be ad-libbed, though not necessarily unprepared.

1. *Interviews.* The introduction, conclusion, and a list of provocative questions can be prepared in advance. When you are interviewing somebody, however, many of your most interesting questions will probably be ad-libbed in response to the answers. If you are being interviewed, your answers should sound spontaneous, but you may think about them ahead of time without selecting the exact words. You can plan to tell about shooting the rapids on the Colorado

River—how you made up your mind to go, what you took with you, the most exciting moment, and what you saw—without composing the sentences you will use.

2. *Demonstrations.* In this type of program, a scripted introduction, conclusion, and a run-down of the sequence of events will help both the performer and the technical staff. For instance, if you're going to demonstrate how to make a kite, the script might include (*a*) the introduction, about the fun of flying a kite along the lake front on a windy day; (*b*) a list of parts needed to make the kite—paper, balsa wood, scissors, glue, string, pattern; (*c*) the order in which you will assemble the parts—lay paper on table, lay pattern on paper, and cut paper on outside pattern lines; (*d*) the conclusion, during which you plan to show the completed kite with a still-photo of a similar kite in flight.

3. *Play-by-play sportscasts.* Sportscasters always have with them certain details about each athlete. If an eligible end receives a forward pass for a gain that may make a first down, the sportscaster has background material on both the quarterback and the end, which can be used while the officials are bringing the chain in from the sidelines to measure the yardage. Fill-ins for every time-out, narration for half-time activities, questions for interviews, lead-ins for every commercial and every station break can all be scripted in advance. If you think a sportscaster needs no script, pay a visit to the booth where the play-by-play is done, and you'll see how he or she manages simultaneously to watch the field, watch three or four monitors, read notes from the spotters, shuffle cards telling about the players' background, and follow instructions from the director!

4. *Game shows.* The M.C. or the announcer always has a script, with an introduction, a conclusion, a lead-in for each commercial, a specific introduction for each player who has been selected in advance, and questions to ask players chosen on the spot. The nature of the game determines whether or not there are cards with questions and answers, scoring regulations, comments to be made to winners, comments to be made to losers, activities or stunts to be performed, or equipment to be manipulated. Much of the content of a game show must be ad-libbed, but there is usually a sequence that you will be aware of if you watch the show regularly.

Which parts of your show should be scripted in advance depend upon the difficulty of the camera work and the skill of the camera operators, the ad-libbing experience of the performers, and the nature of the message to be conveyed.

Suppose, for instance, that as a candidate for an office in your student council, you are to give a five-minute speech on closed-circuit television. You might want to have your campaign manager introduce you with a one-minute description of your qualifications (which might sound conceited coming from you). Then you would devote three of the five minutes to your platform, including proposals to improve the council. After that, you give the editor of the school paper one-and-a-half minutes to ask you one or two questions before you conclude with a 30-second slogan that crystallizes your point of view.

How to Prepare the Script

Whether the script is a verbatim account of what is to be said or a run-down outline of the sequence of events with some dialogue, certain practices should be followed in preparing it.

1. The script should be typed double-spaced on typewriter-size paper, which should be as soft as possible to prevent rattling. Type on one side only.
2. If the script will be visible to viewers, it should be typed on pale-colored paper (blue or green), not white.
3. Pages should be numbered in the upper righthand corner. Although this is not always done, it is most helpful to number the lines. Valuable rehearsal time can be saved if everyone can quickly locate a spot by reference to "line 12 on page 4."
4. Sentences should be completed on the same page on which they begin. Carryovers require turning or sliding pages in the middle of a sentence.
5. Dialogue is typed in upper and lower case.
6. All audio cues (other than speech) and music cues are typed in capital letters. For additional ease of identification, they may be underlined.
7. Directions to performers (e.g., WALK TO THE DOOR) are in capital letters and enclosed in parentheses.

8. Video instructions usually indicate shots by capital letters (e.g., LS, CU, TCU) contrasting with lower-case letters for directions (e.g., dolly in).
9. Pages should be clipped together in such a way that they can be separated easily during rehearsal if desired.
10. During rehearsals, copies of the script should be available to the talent, the director, production assistants, audio technician, technical director, switcher, floor manager, and engineer, even though not all these staff members will need or want copies during the performance.
11. Have two or three extra copies for the files.

Ready to fade up #1
Ready to open ann mike
Ready to cue anncr
Stand by - - 5 sec

fade up #1	TITLE CARD	1.	ANNCR: ↑"Big Ten Roundtable"
open mike	"BIG TEN ROUNDTABLE" *Camera #1*		
Cue anncr		2.	
Ready to cue music			
	Cue music	3.	MUSIC: ↑THEME (COLLEGE SONGS,
	Ready to fade under	4.	DECCA 1567, SIDE 1, CUT 3,
	Ready to cue anncr	5.	↑UP AND FADE UNDER AND OUT)
	fade under		
	Ready to cut to #2	6.	ANNCR: ↑This afternoon Big Ten
	cue anncr		
Cue of ANNCR - #2		7.	Roundtable brings you
	Ready to cut to #1	8.	four debaters from Ohio
	Ready to flip card		
	flip card	9.	State University and
	Cut to #1	10.	Northwestern University. ↑
Cue flip #1 - CONGRESS		11.	They will discuss a proposal
etc #1		12.	currently being considered
Camera #2. DOLLY OUT		13.	by the U. S. Senate. The
TO MS OF JOE WMS.		14.	proposal, a plan for a guaranteed
		15.	annual wage, is not only being
		16.	discussed by Congressmen,
		17.	welfare workers, and taxpayers,
		18.	but by college students as well.
		19.	We wonder why students are so
	Ready to cut to #2	20.	concerned over an issue which
		21.	only indirectly concerns them. ↑
	Cut to #2	22.	Joe Williams, as a member of the
MS - Joe WMS.		23.	Ohio State debate squad, would you
		24.	mind telling us why you are so
		25.	concerned over this particular issue
		26.	at this time in your life?

The following page was taken from a typical script for a television interview program. The handwritten instructions were added by the director during rehearsal, in preparation for the final production.

Variations in the form of a script. The form of the script varies according to the kind of studio in which you are working. In a television laboratory course, where the director is another student, you may need to insert in your script the kind of shot you want at a certain point, and let the director decide which camera will get that shot. For production class projects, you may want to use a script similar to this one for a student demonstration of microphones.

Video	Audio
MS of Leon wearing lavaliere mike	LEON: Description of the lavaliere mike and when it is used.
CU of lavaliere showing on-off switch	LEON: ". . . some lavalieres have on-off switches, which the talent can turn on and off at will if he or she wishes to engage in some vigorous physical
Back to HS shot of Leon	activity."

Note that the script is divided into two columns. The left, or video, column describes what the viewer will see; the right, or audio, column describes what the viewer will hear. The video column describes the camera shot in the usual abbreviated form: MS—a medium or waist-up shot of the talent; CU—a close-up shot of the lavaliere mike switch; and HS—a head-and-shoulders shot of the performer. In this same column, the director will write the number of the camera and the kind of lens he or she wants to use for each of these three shots.

In the audio column, note the general summary of what the talent will say. This is followed by a statement in quotation marks, which indicate that these are the exact words that the speaker will use as a cue for the close-up shot. The underlined words and arrow leading from the audio column to the video indicate that, as the speaker says "have on-off switches," the director will switch to a close-up shot of the lavaliere mike switch. The arrow at the end of the quotation indicates that after the word "activity" the director will go to a head-and-shoulders shot of the speaker, Leon.

Timing.   Scripts also show timing. "Front timing" gives the hours, minutes and seconds from the beginning of the show to the point indicated at the end of either segments or pages. (1:15:00 in timing segments or length of program means 1 hour, 15 minutes, 0 seconds; in clock or schedule timing it means "at exactly 15 seconds after 1:00 o'clock.") At any time during the show, therefore, one can tell at a glance if it is running too fast or getting behind time. Timing may be recorded at the left or at the right, according to the preference of the director.

For instance, if you are televising a commencement program that begins at 8:00 P.M. and is due to be concluded within two hours, your front timing run-down sheet might look like this.

Video	Audio	Timing
This column would include the camera shots, such as LS of seniors entering Field House; CU of a few seniors; pan across row of parents in balcony; CU of more seniors, etc.	Orchestra: *Pomp and Circumstance*	8:00
	Dr. Jones: Invocation	8:20
	Star Spangled Banner	8:23
	Introduction of Plat-form Guests	8:26
	Special Number by A Cappella Choir	8:30
	Introduction of Senior Officers	8:35

This column shows at what time an event should begin if all is running on schedule.

The processional should be over and the seniors in their places by 8:20. The invocation and the *Star-Spangled Banner* should have concluded by 8:26. If the processional is still going on at 8:25, you know some kind of time adjustment will have to be made later in the program if you are to get off the air in time for the 10 (11) o'clock news.

Front timing may also be applied to the total amount of time allotted to the program rather than just to the 8:00–10:00 P.M. slot. If, for example, that same commencement program is being taped for use later, or if you have all the time you want, the timing column might read like this:

Video	Audio	Timing
	Orchestra Pro-cessional	00:00
	Dr. Jones	00:20
	Star-Spangled Banner	00:23
	Introduction of Plat-form Guests	00:26
	Special Number by A Cappella Choir	00:30
	Introduction of Senior Officers	00:35

This column shows how much time has been used up to the point indicated.

If you have been holding a stopwatch on these proceedings, you will know that when the choir begins to sing, the program has already been going on for 30 minutes.

"Back timing" means timing the program from the end to the beginning. The back-timing column lists, at the point indicated, the amount of time remaining until the end of the show. Suppose, for instance, you have one and a half hours allotted for this same commencement program. The back-timing column would look something like this:

Video	Audio	Timing
	Orchestra Pro-cessional	1:30
	Dr. Jones: Invocation	1:15
	Star-Spangled Banner	1:13
	Introduction of Plat-form Guests	1:10
	Special Number by A Cappella Choir	1:05
	Introduction of Senior Officers	1:00
	Welcome by Senior President	0:55
	Address by Prof. Einstein	0:50

This column shows how much time you have left in your 1½ hours.

If Professor Einstein begins his address with only 50 minutes of time remaining, you know that you will probably have to fade out during the recessional or even before the professor has completed his remarks.

In a partially scripted show, with only the introduction and conclusion written out, the segments can be timed and recorded on the script. An arrangement like the one on the following page gives the run-down of a pep rally to be televised by including known time segments and estimating the unknowns.

Video	Audio	Segment time	Running time
	Band	2:00	2:00
	Introduction of Coach and Players	5:00	7:00
	Interview with Coach	3:00	10:00
	Cheers	3:00	13:00
	Announcements re Game Tickets	1:30	14:30
	Credits, Sign-off Station I.D.	0:30	15:00

The segment time is the amount of time each section is expected to take; the running time is cumulative. By the end of the cheering, for example, you should have used up 13 minutes. Most 15-minute programs are timed at 14:30 to allow time for station breaks.

Students in school are often conditioned to follow classroom clocks, even if the sweep second hand jerks sporadically. If so, it may be more helpful to prepare a timing schedule like this one for a show beginning at 9:25 A.M.

Video	Audio	Segment time	Clock
	Band	2:00	9:25–9:27
	Introduction of Basketball Coach and Players	5:00	9:27–9:32
	Interview with Coach	3:00	9:32–9:35
	Cheers	3:00	9:35–9:38

Sometimes, in class laboratory productions, there is a tendency to be lax about strict timing, but such laxity tends to become a habit. In commercial television in any station that is actually broadcasting, the timing of the programs, station breaks, commercials, and sign-offs is strictly adhered to. So begin by becoming time-conscious. You can soon learn to judge how long a paragraph will take, or a sentence, or a scene. In television, there is no such thing as an excused tardiness, an early dismissal, or an overtime period. Write with the clock in mind.

Clearance and copyright.   If you are preparing your script for a classroom studio presentation within your school building, the problems of clearance (that is, permission to use copyrighted material) will be minimal. Even so, you must obtain permission to distribute, via closed circuit, a film that your school has rented or purchased to project in the auditorium.

Familiarity with some of the basic regulations for clearance of copyright material may avoid trouble. For example, a local radio station arranged for the remote broadcast of a school band program during the weekly assembly. The musical selections were submitted to the station for clearance, and everything seemed under control until the morning of the broadcast, when the trumpet soloist became ill. The band leader had to rearrange the program, substituting a number which had not been cleared for broadcast, and in the last-minute excitement failed to notify the station of the change. When the director at the station heard the number introduced, he quickly called for a switch from remote to the studio. Parents listening in had no idea why, in the middle of the band concert, they heard, "We switch you now to our downtown studio for an interlude of recorded music," and two-and-a-half minutes later, "We return you now to Merrill Auditorium for the band concert already in progress." That was radio. What would have happened if it had been a television program?

Reproductions of copyrighted pictures, recorded music, and published literary selections are protected by copyright laws. You must obtain permission to use these materials for most radio or television broadcasts. Most commercial stations have contracts with the major organizations that hold music copyrights; BMI (Broadcast Music Incorporated), ASCAP (American Society of Composers, Authors, Publishers), and SESAC (Society of European Stage Authors and Composers).

The stations agree by contract to pay a lump sum for the presentation of copyrighted music. Your responsibility is to submit to the station, in advance, the titles, composers, arrangers, and publishers of all musical numbers to be included in your program. If you plan to quote poetry or sing a song as you crown the homecoming queen during the telecast of a football game, or if your school plans a special half-time program of copyrighted music, avoid any possible difficulties by giving the station advance notice. Don't place your school or the cooperating station in an embarrassing situation by failing to comply with copyright regulations. Being 100 percent honest about the use of restricted material is a good habit to get into if you plan to do any programs on a commercial station. Even though your script may seem to be limited by the need for clearing copyrighted material, even though you may feel that your basic freedom of speech is being restricted, you are really just asking permission to use something that belongs to another person.

Television Code.   Verbalizing your message will be further restricted when you prepare script copy for a commercial station, for the television industry has a strict self-regulatory code of ethics. If you are preparing a script for one of approximately four hundred stations that subscribe to the Television Code, your copy would have to meet the program and advertising standards these stations have set up to regulate themselves. The Code subscriber stations, whose seal you see displayed as the station goes on and off the air each day, are monitored for their compliance with provisions for the total amount of advertising material in a program as well as the number of interruptions and the general objectives of truth, safety, fairness, and good taste. The standards of programming do not indicate specifically what should or should not be aired; rather, they are an interpretation of what is meant by "broadcasting in the public interest, convenience, and necessity." Single copies of the Television Code may be obtained from the Code Authority, National Association of Broadcasters, 1771 N Street NW, Washington, D.C. 20036.

The Code guidelines used to check script for program content include these few examples.

1. Profanity, obscenity, smut, and vulgarity are forbidden, even when likely to be understood only by part of the au-

dience. From time to time, words that have been acceptable, acquire undesirable meanings, and telecasters should be alert to eliminate such words.

2. Words (especially slang) derisive of any race, color, creed, nationality or national derivation, except wherein such usage would be for the specific purpose of effective dramatization, such as combating prejudice, are forbidden. . . .

3. The presentation of techniques of crime in such detail as to invite imitation shall be avoided.

4. The creation of a state of hypnosis by act or demonstration on the air is prohibited, and hypnosis as an aspect of "parlor game" antics to create humorous situations within comedy situations cannot be used.

Other content areas covered by the guidelines include ridicule of racial or nationality types; attacks on religion and religious faiths; reference to physical or mental afflictions and deformities; law enforcement; legal, medical, and other professional advice, diagnosis, and treatment; use of animals; use of gambling devices; on-the-scene betting at sports events; quiz shows; horror shows; lottery contests; and such expletives as "flash" or "bulletin" (to avoid a repetition of the famous Orson Welles radio show, which was interpreted as an actual newscast reporting the landing of men from another planet); treatment of news and special public events; controversial public issues; and political telecasts.

In scripts for your school telecasts, you will not be concerned with the Code's regulations for advertising, but if you ever write copy for a commercial station or advertising agency, you will have to meet certain restrictions on the content and time of all TV advertising. Study this brief sample of advertising regulations from the Code, and then check some of the commercials you watch on television to see whether they comply.

1. "Children's program hosts or primary cartoon characters shall not be utilized to deliver commercial messages within or adjacent to the programs which feature such hosts or cartoon characters."

2. In commercials for services or over-the-counter products involving health considerations, "physicians, dentists or nurses, or actors representing physicians, dentists or nurses, shall not be employed directly or by implication." Surely you

have seen at least one commercial which does not comply
with this!

3. "In prime time on network affiliated stations non-program
    material (that is, advertising) shall not exceed 9 minutes, 30
    seconds in any 60-minute period. . . . On independent sta-
    tions non-program material shall not exceed 12 minutes in
    any 60-minute period."

4. "In prime time the number of program interruptions shall
    not exceed 2 within any 30-minute program or 4 within any
    60-minute program."

5. "In children's week-end time . . . the number of program
    interruptions shall not exceed 2 within any 30-minute pro-
    gram or 4 within any 60-minute program."

6. "No more than 4 non-program material announcements
    shall be scheduled consecutively within programs, and no
    more than 3 non-program material announcements shall be
    scheduled consecutively during station breaks." The word
    "consecutively" gives the station the chance to schedule
    three ads, then a station break, then three more ads between
    programs.

7. A 9" × 12" wall sign or a 3" × 10" desk sign giving the name
    of the sponsor or product may be displayed during the pro-
    gram portion of the show. During a baseball telecast spon-
    sored by a gasoline company a sign on a large billboard
    advertising another brand of gasoline caused much con-
    troversy about compliance.

The station and its cooperating advertisers, through television, visit most of the homes in America, including people of all
ages, backgrounds, beliefs, and standards of conduct. The
revenue from advertising enables the American system of broadcasting to provide the finest programs of information and entertainment as well as programs of lower quality. If you occasionally become disillusioned with the quality of a program or the
good taste of its advertisements, you have a responsibility to express your views and make constructive suggestions. Write your
local station or one of the three major networks, and send a copy
of your letter to the Code Authority.

American Broadcasting Company   Columbia Broadcasting System
1330 Avenue of the Americas   51 West 52nd Street
New York, N.Y. 10019   New York, N.Y. 10019

National Broadcasting Company
30 Rockefeller Plaza
New York, N.Y. 10020

Public Broadcasting Service
485 L'Enfante Plaza West, S.W.
Washington, D.C. 20024
Television Code Authority
National Association of Broadcasters
1771 N St., N.W.
Washington, D.C. 20036

If you complain about a specific program, include the time and date it is shown, also the network, city, station call letters, and channel number, in addition to stating what you consider objectionable.

Evaluating the script.   Finally, after writing your script, check your copy with these questions.

1. Do I begin in an attention-getting way—to keep listeners from turning off a school program?
2. Overall, what message am I trying to get across to the viewers?
3. Are my picture statements matching the content from audio?
4. Have I selected content that will convey my message?
5. Have I chosen words that will communicate my meaning to the kind of people who will be watching local television at noon on a weekday? Will my vocabulary turn them on or off?
6. Have I assumed that viewers understand activities and terminology peculiar to my school? If I mention "poli-sci" or a "bull session," can I assume they know what I mean?
7. What pictures are needed to make the ideas clear?
8. Have I prepared the script in correct form? (See pages 150–151).
9. Have I checked my graphics for 4 × 3 aspect ratio, for legibility, for neatness, and professional appearance?
10. Have I provided a *cushion*?
11. Will this content be acceptable to the Television Code?
12. Is the program, as it appears in my script, worth spending time to produce and present?

If it is true that "one picture is worth a thousand words," the television scriptwriter has an obligation to see that the words used add to and emphasize, rather than detract from, the impact of the visual message.

Take Two

1. Why would a television newscast require a complete script for the director and talent?

2. Imagine you are the producer or host of a local talk show. Think of ten questions that would be needed for the following guests:
    a. Mayor or manager of your town or city
    b. Your football or basketball coach
    c. The program director of the local radio station
    d. Principal of your school
    e. Student council president

3. Why is it not a good idea for a beginning television performer to memorize his or her speech or use cue cards instead of a script?

4. What is the difference between back timing and front timing. Set up an imaginary 15 minute newscast, and determine the running time for each story or sequence.

5. What is the function of ASCAP or BMI?

6. What is the difference between the National Association "Code" and the FCC Rules?

7. Why does the NAB Code insist that hosts of children's shows "not be utilized to deliver commercial messages in the program?"

1. Assume that a local cable television service has given your school five minutes of a thirty-minute newscast at noon. For this occasion, write a five-minute script that you will present on camera. For musical background, you may use a recording of your school song. The station has limited you to three graphics, exclusive of the title cards that it furnishes. You may include a two-minute live interview with a guest from school, either a student or a staff member. Check your script by answering these questions.

    a. Which of my news stories will need pictures to make them clear?

    b. Have I made a clear distinction between statements of fact and my commentary

    c. Have I cleared the use of pictures with the director?

    d. Have I cleared music and music cues?

    e. Have I checked statements of fact to verify their accuracy? Is the new Boosters Club president Mrs. T. *Ellsworth* Brown or Mrs. T. *Ellison* Brown?

    f. Have I timed the script with a stopwatch and recorded the time for the director?

    g. If I have included an interview, has that segment been timed—with alternative questions and if-cuts to be used to meet timing cues?

    h. Have I cleared all copyrighted material?

    If your school has a videotape recorder, have your newscast recorded and play it back for self-criticism. Be honest as you watch it. Would you turn it off if it weren't your own program? What message does it convey about the kind of school you attend, about what's going on there, about your integrity as a reporter, about you as a person?

2. Imagine you are the producer of a local interview program. The program opens with a title card or key title. A host introduces the program and brings out the first guest, who talks for a few minutes with the host and then either demonstrates his or her hobby or performs by singing,

dancing, playing an instrument, or reading literature. After the performance, the guest returns and the host asks a few more questions before closing the program with the announcement of future guests. The program closes with music and a closing title or key card. The format is

a.   Opening titles and music
b.   Host introduces program and guest
c.   Guest demonstrates or performs
d.   Host and guest talk
e.   Host wraps up
f.   Closing titles and music.

Write a script that will allow for flexibility and yet will make this work. You will need at least two copies (one for the director and one for the host). Set up a floor plan for this program, and produce the program on video tape for analysis.

3.   Write a script for a 15-minute show during which you, as M.C., interview the coach, co-captains, and head cheerleader on the Wednesday before the basketball tournament weekend. Check the content of your script with these questions.

a.   Have I done my "homework" well by obtaining facts, human-interest items, significant details, and correct statistics on records and events?

b.   Do I have a tantalizing introduction that will make viewers want to stay tuned?

c.   Do I have well-phrased transitions to lead from the cheerleader to the co-captains and from the co-captains to the assistant coach? Have I prepared substitute statements for "Next we have . . ."?

d.   Do I have questions that will give the coach a chance to say what he or she needs and wants to say, or have I bottled him or her up with yes and no questions?

e.   Have I made it easy for the co-captains to make comments without embarrassment? Have I kidded too much?

f.   Are all my questions the same old trite ones, starting with "How did you feel when . . .?" or do I include some penetrating queries that will elicit refreshing viewpoints on this particular sports event?

g.   Are all my questions worded in such a way that the interviewee will know what I mean and won't appear stupid as he or she attempts to answer?

h.   Do my questions sound as if I have been listening to the answers?

i.   What comments do I make after an answer? "Oh, I see" may be excused once but not more than that.

j.   Am I trying to get across the same message as the coach and co-captains?

k.   Have I though of my viewers, and tried to ask questions they would like to ask?

Check the form of the script with these questions.

a.   Have I used capital letters to distinguish speakers' names, directions, camera shots, music, and sound effects?

b.   Have I used arrows and/or underlining to indicate to the technical staff the exact word cue when some action is to take place?

c.   Is it clear how much time I expect each segment to take?

d.   Are the if-cuts clearly marked to indicate passages I may need to omit?

e.   Have I included alternative endings, with the exact times indicated, to enable me to conclude exactly on cue?

f.   Have I given credit for using other people's material?

g.   Have I cleared the music I wish to use?

4.   Take a cutting of 4-6 minutes from a scene in a play and adapt it for television. You might use the standard video and audio television script form. Many modern plays will work for this exercise. Some interesting plays include *Odd Couple, Barefoot in the Park, Inherit the Wind, Our Town,* and many other modern plays. Work in small groups. First, write the script using the television format, design and secure a simple set. Often just simple set furniture will work for this exercise. Find costumes and props needed for the production, light the set, and produce this play, cutting for television.

5.   Freedom of speech (interpreted by the media to include the right to know and hear) is currently a most controversial issue. The relation between censorship and the granting of licences, the manipulation and protection of news sources, and the right of an individual to have a fair trial with all the pre-trial publicity (often aired on radio and television) are issues that are important to everyone interested in keeping our press free. Create some panel discussions on some of the following topics regarding fair trial, free press, and other topics.

a. Can a person in a famous criminal trial actually obtain an impartial jury with all the background obtained by radio and television before the trial starts? (Read Gannett Co. Inc. vs DePasquale, 1979.)

b. Does a reporter have the right to keep informants secret, even if the information is important in court procedings? (Read Branzburg vs. Hayse, 1972 before Supreme Court.)

c. Should radio and television stations have to offer "equal time" for all political candidates as specified by the FCC rules?

6. Write a script for a 15-minute children's show.

7. Some situation comedy series begin "cold." They open with dialogue and an incident, omitting any announcements. Following this "open cold," the credits and announcements are presented and the show proceeds. An "open cold" is a good way to let the audience know what the story will be about. Read the script at the end of this chapter and try to write an "open cold" that will give one minute of dialogue to set the stage for what happens in the script. Watch a few situation comedies to see how many use this kind of opening.

8. The National Association of Broadcasters specifies the amount of commercial time that should be observed by member stations. To see if stations in your area conform to the code, use a stopwatch and time the exact amount of commercial messages aired during one hour of prime time. See if this time meets the NAB Code.

9. Write a segment for *Sesame Street*, using the same characters as the original show, but following your own plot line.

10. Take one of your favorite short stories and adapt it for a television production, in the format of narration with pantomime, a play, a puppet show, or in some other format you wish to try.

11. Read *The Monsters Are Due on Maple Street*, a script from the *Twilight Zone* television series by award winning writer, Rod Serling, whose stories were also seen on the *Night Gallery* series. Notice how Mr. Serling told an exciting, suspenseful story that verbalized a message about suspicion, prejudice, violence, and pressure. (*Script follows.*)

Rewrite the form of the script using video and audio columns. In the video column, write the camera directions you would use in staging this play with the cameras and equipment you have available in your school's television studio.

The Monsters Are Due on Maple Street

by Rod Serling

CHARACTERS

Narrator

Figure One

Figure Two

Residents of Maple Street:

    Don Martin

    Steve Brand

    Myra Brand, Steve's wife

    Pete Van Horn

Charlie

Charlie's Wife

Tommy

Sally, Tommy's Mother

Les Goodman

Ethel Goodman, Les's Wife

Man One

Woman One

Woman Two

ACT ONE

SCENE 1. *(FADE IN ONE SHOT OF THE NIGHT SKY. The various heavenly bodies stand out in sharp, sparkling relief. As the CAMERA begins a SLOW PAN across the heavens, we hear the narrator.)*

NARRATOR *(off stage):* There is a fifth dimension beyond that which is known to man. It is a dimension as vast as space, and as timeless as infinity. It is the middle ground between light and shadow—between science and superstition. And it lies between the pit of man's fears and the summit of his knowledge. This is the dimension of imagination. It is an area which we call the Twilight Zone.

SCENE 2. *(THE CAMERA BEGINS TO PAN DOWN until it passes the horizon and stops on a sign which reads "Maple Street." It is daytime. Then we see the street below. It is a quiet, tree-lined, small-town American street. The houses have front porches on which people sit and swing on gliders, talking across from house to house. STEVE BRAND is polishing his car, which is parked in front of his house. His neighbor, DON MARTIN, leans against the fender watching him. A Good Humor man riding his bicycle is just in the process of stopping to sell some ice cream to a couple of kids. Two women gossip on the front lawn. Another man is watering his lawn with a garden hose.*

At this moment TOMMY, one of the two boys buying ice cream from the vendor, looks up to listen to a tremendous screeching roar from overhead. A flash of light plays on the faces of both boys and then moves down the street and disappears.

Various people leave their porches or stop what they are doing to stare up at the sky.

Steve Brand, the man who has been polishing his car, stands there transfixed, staring upwards. He looks at Don Martin, his neighbor from across the street.)

STEVE: What was that? A meteor?

DON: That's what it looked like. I didn't hear any crash though, did you?

STEVE: Nope. I didn't hear anything except a roar.

MRS. BRAND *(from her porch):* Steve? What was that?

STEVE *(raising his voice and looking toward the porch):* Guess it was a meteor, honey. Came awful close, didn't it?

MRS. BRAND: Too close for my money! Much too close.

(THE CAMERA PANS ACROSS THE VARIOUS PORCHES to people who stand there watching and talking in low conversing tones.)

NARRATOR: Maple Street. Six-forty-four P.M. on a late September evening. *(A pause)* Maple Street in the last calm and reflective moment . . . before the monsters came!

(THE CAMERA TAKES US ACROSS THE PORCHES AGAIN. A man is screwing a light bulb on a front porch. He gets down off his stool to flick the switch and finds that nothing happens.

Another man is working on an electric power mower. He plugs in the plug, flicks the switch of the mower off and on, but nothing happens.

Through a window we see a woman pushing her finger back and forth on the dial hook of a telephone. Her voice sounds far away.)

WOMAN ONE: Operator, operator, something's wrong on the phone, operator!

(Mrs. Brand comes out on the porch and calls to Steve.)

MRS. BRAND *(calling):* Steve, the power's off. I had the soup on the stove and the stove just stopped working.

WOMAN ONE: Same thing over here. I can't get anybody on the phone either. The phone seems to be dead.

(We look down again on the street. Small, mildly disturbed voices creep up from below.)

VOICE ONE: Electricity's off.

VOICE TWO: Phone won't work.

VOICE THREE: Can't get a thing on the radio.

VOICE FOUR: My power mower won't move, won't work at all.

VOICE FIVE: Radio's gone dead!

(Pete Van Horn, a tall, thin man, is seen standing in front of his house.)

VAN HORN: I'll cut through the back yard . . . see if the power's still on on Floral Street. I'll be right back!

(He walks past the side of his house and disappears into the back yard.

THE CAMERA PANS DOWN SLOWLY until we are looking at ten or eleven people standing around the street and overflowing to the curb and sidewalk. In the background is Steve Brand's car.)

STEVE: Doesn't make sense. Why should the power go off all of a sudden *and* the phone line?

DON: Maybe some kind of an electrical storm or something.

CHARLIE: That don't seem likely. Sky's just as blue as anything. Not a cloud. No lightning. No thunder. No nothing. How could it be a storm?

WOMAN ONE: I can't get a thing on the radio. Not even the portable.

(The people again murmur softly in wonderment.)

CHARLIE: Well, why don't you go downtown and check with the police, though they'll probably think we're crazy or something. A little power failure and right away we get all flustered and everything—

STEVE: It isn't just the power failure, Charlie. If it was, we'd still be able to get a broadcast on the portable.

(There is a murmur of reaction to this. Steve looks from face to face and then over to his car.)

STEVE: I'll run downtown. We'll get this all straightened out.

(He walks over to the car, gets in, and turns the key.

Looking through the open car door, we see the crowd watching Steve from the other side. He starts the engine. It turns over sluggishly and then stops dead. He tries it again, and this time he can't get it to turn over. Then very slowly he turns the key back to "off" and gets out of the car.

The people stare at Steve. He stands for a moment by the car and then walks toward them.)

STEVE: I don't understand it. It was working fine before—

DON: Out of gas?

STEVE *(shakes his head):* I just had it filled up.

WOMAN ONE: What's it mean?

CHARLIE: It's just as if . . . as if everything had stopped. *(Then he turns toward Steve.)* We'd better *walk* downtown.

(Another murmur of assent to this.)

STEVE: The two of us can go, Charlie. *(He turns to look back at the car.)* It couldn't be the meteor. A meteor couldn't do *this*.

(He and Charlie exchange a look. Then they start to walk away from the group.

Tommy comes into view. He is a serious-faced young boy in spectacles. He stands halfway between the group and the two men who start to walk down the sidewalk.)

TOMMY: Mr. Brand . . . you'd better not!

STEVE: Why not?

TOMMY: They don't want you to.

(Steve and Charlie exchange a grin and Steve looks back toward the boy.)

STEVE: *Who* doesn't want us to?

TOMMY: *(jerks his head in the general direction of the distant horizon):* Them!

STEVE: Them?

CHARLIE: Who are them?

TOMMY *(intently):* Whoever was in that thing that came by overhead.

Steve knits his brows for a moment, cocking his head questioningly. His voice is intense.)

STEVE: What?

TOMMY: Whoever was in that thing that came over. I don't think they want us to leave here.

(Steve leaves Charlie, walks over to the boy, and puts his hand on the boy's shoulder. He forces his voice to remain gentle.)

STEVE: What do you mean? What are you talking about?

TOMMY: They don't want us to leave. That's why they shut everything off.

STEVE: What makes you say that? Whatever gave you *that* idea?

WOMAN ONE *(from the crowd):* Now isn't that the craziest thing you ever heard?

TOMMY *(persistent but a little frightened):* It's always that way, in every story I ever read about a ship landing from outer space.

WOMAN ONE *(to the boy's mother, Sally, who stands on the fringe of the crowd):* From outer space yet! Sally, you better get that boy of yours up to bed. He's been reading too many comic books or seeing too many movies or something!

SALLY: Tommy, come over here and stop that kind of talk.

STEVE: Go ahead, Tommy. We'll be right back. And you'll see. That wasn't any ship or anything like it. That was just a . . . a meteor or something. Likely as not—*(He turns to the group, now trying very hard to sound more optimistic than he feels.)* No doubt it did have something to do with all this power failure and the rest of it. Meteors can do some crazy things. Like sun spots.

DON *(picking up the cue):* Sure. That's the kind of thing—like sun spots. They raise Cain with radio reception all over the world. And this thing being so close—why, there's no telling the sort of stuff it can do. *(He wets his lips, smiles nervously.)* Go ahead, Charlie. You and Steve go into town and see if that isn't what's causing it all.

(Steve and Charlie walk away from the group down the sidewalk as the people watch silently.

Tommy stares at them, biting his lips, and finally calls out again.)

TOMMY: Mr. Brand!

(The two men stop. Tommy takes a step toward them.)

TOMMY: Mr. Brand . . . please don't leave here.

(Steve and Charlie stop once again and turn toward the boy. In the crowd there is a murmur of irritation and concern, as if the boy's words—even though they didn't make sense—were bringing up fears that shouldn't be brought up.

Tommy is partly frightened and partly defiant.)

TOMMY: You might not even be able to get to town. It was that way in the story. *Nobody* could leave. Nobody except—

STEVE: Except who?

TOMMY: Except the people they'd sent down ahead of them. They looked just like humans. And it wasn't until the ship landed that—*(The boy suddenly stops, conscious of the people staring at him and his mother and of the sudden hush of the crowd.)*

SALLY *(in a whisper, sensing the antagonism of the crowd):* Tommy, please son . . . honey, don't talk that way—

MAN ONE: That kid shouldn't talk that way . . . and we shouldn't stand here listening to him. Why, this is the craziest thing I ever heard of. The kid tells us a comic book plot and here we stand listening—

(Steve walks toward the camera, and stops beside the boy.)

STEVE: Go ahead, Tommy. What kind of story was this? What about the people they sent out ahead?

TOMMY: That was the way they prepared things for the landing. They sent four people. A mother and a father and two kids who looked just like humans . . . but they weren't.

(There is another silence as Steve looks toward the crowd and then toward Tommy. He wears a tight grin.)

STEVE: Well, I guess what we'd better do then is to run a check on the neighborhood and see which ones of us are really human.

(There is laughter at this, but it's a laughter that comes from a desperate attempt to lighten the atmosphere. The people look at one another in the middle of their laughter.)

CHARLIE *(rubs his jaw nervously):* I wonder if Floral Street's got the same deal we got. *(He looks past the houses.)* Where is Pete Van Horn anyway? Didn't he get back yet?

(Suddenly there is the sound of a car's engine starting to turn over.

WE LOOK ACROSS THE STREET TOWARD THE DRIVEWAY OF LES GOODMAN'S HOUSE. He is at the wheel trying to start the car.)

SALLY: Can you get started, Les?

(Les Goodman gets out of the car, shaking his head.)

GOODMAN: No dice.

(He walks toward the group. He stops suddenly as, behind him, the car engine starts up all by itself. Goodman whirls around to stare at it.

The car idles roughly, smoke coming from the exhaust, the frame shaking gently.

Goodman's eyes go wide, and he runs over to his car.

The people stare at the car.)

MAN ONE: He got the car started somehow. He got *his* car started!

(The people continue to stare, caught up by this revelation and wildly frightened.)

WOMAN ONE: How come his car just up and started like that?

SALLY: All by itself. He wasn't anywheres near it. It started all by itself.

(Don Martin approaches the group, stops a few feet away to look toward Goodman's car and then back toward the group.)

DON: And he never did come out to look at that thing that flew overhead. He wasn't even interested. *(He turns to the group, his face taut and serious.)* Why? Why didn't he come out with the rest of us to look?

CHARLIE: He always was an odd ball. Him and his whole family. Real odd ball.

DON: What do you say we ask him?

(The group start toward the house. In this brief fraction of a moment they take the first step toward a metamorphosis that changes people from a group into a mob. They begin to head purposefully across the street toward the house. Steve stands in front of them. For a moment their fear almost turns their walk into a wild stampede, but Steve's voice, loud, incisive, and commanding, makes them stop.)

STEVE: Wait a minute . . . *wait a minute!* Let's not be a mob!

(The people stop, pause for a moment . . . and then much more quietly and slowly start to walk across the street.

Goodman stands alone facing the people.)

GOODMAN: I just don't understand it. I tried to start it and it wouldn't start. You saw me. All of you saw me.

(And now, just as suddenly as the engine started, it stops, and there is a long silence that is gradually intruded upon by the frightened murmuring of the people.)

GOODMAN: I don't understand. I swear . . . I don't understand. What's happening?

DON: Maybe you better tell us. Nothing's working on this street. Nothing. No lights, no power, no radio. *(Then meaningfully)* Nothing except one car—yours!

(The people's murmuring becomes a loud chant filling the air with accusations and demands for action. Two of the men pass Don and head toward Goodman who backs away from them against his car. He is cornered.)

GOODMAN: Wait a minute now. You keep your distance—all of you. So I've got a car that starts by itself—well, that's a freak thing—I admit it. But does that make me some kind of a criminal or something? I don't know why the car works—it just does!

(This stops the crowd momentarily and Goodman still backing away goes toward his front porch. He goes up the steps and then stops, facing the mob.)

GOODMAN: What's it all about Steve?

STEVE *(quietly):* We're all on a monster kick, Les. Seems that the general impression holds that maybe one family isn't what we think they are. Monsters from outer space or something. Different from us. Fifth columnists from the vast beyond. *(He chuckles.)* You know anybody that might fit that description around here on Maple Street?

GOODMAN: What is this, a gag? *(He looks around the group again.)* This a practical joke or something?

(Suddenly the car engine starts all by itself, runs for a moment, and stops. One woman begins to cry. The eyes of the crowd are cold and accusing.)

GOODMAN: Now that's supposed to incriminate me, huh? The car engine goes on and off and that really does it, doesn't it? *(He looks around the faces of the people.)* I just don't understand it . . . any more than any of you do! *(He wets his lips, looking from face to face.)* Look, you all know me. We've lived here five years. Right in this house. We're no different from any of the rest of you! We're no different at all . . . Really . . . this whole thing is just weird—

WOMAN ONE: Well, if that's the case. Les Goodman, explain why—*(She stops suddenly, clamping her mouth shut.)*

GOODMAN *(softly):* Explain what?

STEVE *(interjecting):* Look, let's forget this—

CHARLIE *(overlapping him):* Go ahead, let her talk. What about it? Explain what?

WOMAN ONE *(a little reluctantly):* Well . . . sometimes I go to bed late at night. A couple of times . . . a couple of times I'd come out here on the porch and I'd see Mr. Goodman here in the wee hours of the morning standing out in front of his house . . . looking up at the sky. *(She looks around the circle of faces.)* That's right, looking up at the sky as if . . . as if he were waiting for something. *(A pause)* As if he were looking for something.

(There's a murmur of reaction from the crowd again as Goodman backs away.)

GOODMAN: She's crazy. Look, I can explain that. Please . . . I can really explain that . . . she's making it up anyway. *(Then he shouts)* I tell you she's making it up!

(He takes a step toward the crowd and they back away from him. He walks down the steps after them and they continue to back away. Suddenly he is left completely alone, and he looks like a man caught in the middle of a menacing circle as the scene SLOWLY FADES TO BLACK.)

ACT TWO

SCENE 1. *(FADE IN ON MAPLE STREET AT NIGHT. On the sidewalk, little knots of people stand around talking in low voices. At the end of each conversation they look toward Les Goodman's house. From the various houses we can see candlelight but no electricity. The quiet which blankets the whole area is disturbed only by the almost whispered voices of the people standing around. In one group Charlie stands staring across at Goodman's house. Two men stand across the street from it in almost sentry-like poses.)*

SALLY *(in a small, hesitant voice):* It doesn't seem right, though, keeping watch on them. Why . . . he was right when he said he was one of our neighbors. Why, I've known Ethel Goodman ever since they moved in. We've been good friends—

CHARLIE: That don't prove a thing. Any guy who'd spend his time lookin' up at the sky early in the morning—well, there's something wrong with that kind of person. There's something that ain't legitimate. Maybe under normal circumstances we could let it go by, but these aren't normal circumstances. Why, look at this street! Nothin' but candles. Why, it's like goin' back into the dark ages or somethin'!

(Steve walks down the steps of his porch, down the street to Les Goodman's house, and then stops at the foot of the steps. Goodman is standing there; Mrs. Goodman behind him is very frightened.)

GOODMAN: Just stay right where you are, Steve. We don't want any trouble, but this time if anybody sets foot on my porch—that's what they're going to get—trouble.

STEVE: Look, Les—

GOODMAN: I've already explained to you people. I don't sleep very well at night sometimes. I get up and I take a walk and I look up at the sky. I look at the stars!

MRS. GOODMAN: That's exactly what he does. Why, this whole thing, it's . . . it's some kind of madness or something.

STEVE *(nods grimly):* That's exactly what it is—some kind of madness.

CHARLIE'S VOICE *(shrill, from across the street):* You best watch who you're seen with, Steve! Until we get this all straightened out, you ain't exactly above suspicion yourself.

STEVE *(whirling around toward him):* Or you, Charlie. Or any of us, it seems. From age eight on up!

WOMAN ONE: What I'd like to know is—what are we gonna do? Just stand around here all night?

CHARLIE: There's nothin' else we *can* do! *(He turns back, looking toward Steve and Goodman again.)* One of 'em'll tip their hand. They *got* to.

STEVE *(raising his voice):* There's something you can do, Charlie. You can go home and keep your mouth shut. You can quit strutting around like a self-appointed hanging judge and just climb into bed and forget it.

CHARLIE: You sound real anxious to have that happen, Steve. I think we better keep our eye on you, too!

DON *(as if he were taking the bit in his teeth, takes a hesitant step to the front):* I think everything might as well come out now. *(He turns toward Steve.)* Your wife's done plenty of talking, Steve, about how *odd* you are!

CHARLIE *(picking this up, his eyes widening):* Go ahead, tell us what she's said.
(Steve walks toward them from across the street.)

STEVE: Go ahead, what's my wife said?
Let's get it *all* out. Let's pick out every idiosyncrasy of every single man, woman, and child on the street. And then we might as well set up some kind of kangaroo court. How about a firing squad at dawn, Charlie, so we can get rid of all the suspects. Narrow them down..Make it easier for you.

DON: There's no need gettin' so upset, Steve. It's just that . . . well . . . Myra's talked about how there's been plenty of nights you spent hours down in your basement workin' on some kind of radio or something. Well, none of us have ever *seen* that radio—
(By this time Steve has reached the group. He stands there defiantly.)

CHARLIE: Go ahead, Steve. What kind of "radio set" you workin' on? I never seen it. Neither has anyone else. Who you talk to on that radio set? And who talks to you?

STEVE: I'm surprised at you, Charlie. How come you're so dense all of a sudden? *(A pause.)* Who do I talk to? I talk to monsters from outer space. I talk to three-headed green men who fly over here in what look like meteors.
(Mrs. Brand steps down from the porch, bites her lip, calls out.)

MRS. BRAND: Steve! Steve, please. *(Then looking around, frightened, she walks toward the group.)* It's just a ham radio set, that's all. I bought him a book on it myself. It's just a ham radio set. A lot of people have them. I can show it to you. It's right down in the basement.

STEVE *(whirls around toward her):* Show them nothing! If they want to look inside our house—let them get a search warrant.

CHARLIE: Look, buddy, you can't afford to—

STEVE *(interrupting him):* Charlie, don't start telling me who's dangerous and who isn't and who's safe and who's a menace. *(He turns to the group and shouts.)* And you're with him, too—all of you! You're standing here all set to crucify—all set to find a scapegoat—all desperate to point some kind of finger at a neighbor! Well now, look, friends, the only thing that's gonna happen is that we'll eat each other up alive—

(He stops abruptly as Charlie suddenly grabs his arm.)

CHARLIE *(in a hushed voice):* That's not the *only* thing that can happen to us. *(Down the street, a figure has suddenly materialized in the gloom, and in the silence we hear the clickety-clack of slow, measured footsteps on concrete as the figure walks slowly toward them. One of the women lets out a stifled cry. Sally grabs her boy, as do a couple of other mothers.)*

TOMMY *(shouting, frightened):* It's the monster! It's the monster!

(Another woman lets out a wail and the people fall back in a group staring toward the darkness and the approaching figure.

The people stand in the shadows watching. Don Martin joins them, carrying a shotgun. He holds it up.)

DON: We may need this.

STEVE: A shotgun? *(He pulls it out of Don's hand.)* Good Lord—will anybody think a thought around here? Will you people wise up? What good would a shotgun do against—

(The dark figure continues to walk toward them as the people stand there, fearful, mothers clutching children, men standing in front of their wives.)

CHARLIE *(pulling the gun from Steve's hands):* No more talk, Steve. You're going to talk us into a grave! You'd let whatever's out there walk right over us, wouldn't you? Well, some of us won't!

(Charlie swings around, raises the gun, and suddenly pulls the trigger. The sound of the shot explodes in the stillness.

The figure suddenly lets out a small cry, stumbles forward onto his knees, and then falls forward on his face. Don, Charlie, and Steve race forward to him. Steve is there first and turns the man over. The crowd gathers around them.)

STEVE *(slowly looks up):* It's Pete Van Horn.

DON *(in a hushed voice):* Pete Van Horn! He was just gonna go over to the next block to see if the power was on—

WOMAN ONE: You killed him, Charlie. You shot him dead!

CHARLIE *(looks around at the circle of faces, his eyes frightened, his face contorted):* But . . . but I didn't know who he was. I certainly didn't know who he was. He comes walkin' out of the darkness—how am I supposed to know who he was? *(He grabs Steve.)* Steve—you know why I shot! How was I supposed to know he wasn't a monster or something? *(He grabs Don.)* We're all scared of the same thing. I was just tryin' to . . . tryin' to protect my home, that's all! Look, all of you, that's all I was tryin' to do.

(He looks down wildly at the body.) I didn't know it was somebody we knew! I didn't know—

(There's a sudden hush and then an intake of breath in the group. Across the street all the lights go on in one of the houses.)

WOMAN ONE *(in a hushed voice):* Charlie . . . Charlie . . . the lights just went on in your house. Why did the lights just go on?

DON: What about it, Charlie? How come you're the only one with lights now?

GOODMAN: That's what I'd like to know.

(A pause as they all stare toward Charlie.)

GOODMAN: You were so quick to kill, Charlie, and you were so quick to tell us who we had to be careful of. Well, maybe you *had* to kill. Maybe Pete there was trying to tell us something. Maybe he'd found out something and came back to tell us who there was amongst us we should watch out for—

(Charlie backs away from the group, his eyes wide with fright.)

CHARLIE: No . . . no . . . it's nothing of the sort! I don't know why the lights are on. I swear I don't. Somebody's pulling a gag or something.

(He bumps against Steve who grabs him and whirls him around.)

STEVE: A *gag?* A gag? Charlie, there's a dead man on the sidewalk and you killed him! Does this thing look like a gag to you?

(Charlie breaks away and screams as he runs toward his house.)

CHARLIE: No! No! Please!

(A man breaks away from the crowd to chase Charlie.

As the man tackles him and lands on top of him, the other people start to run toward them. Charlie gets up, breaks away from the other man's grasp, lands a couple of desperate punches that push the man aside. Then he forces his way, fighting, through the crowd and jumps up on his front porch.

Charlie is on his porch as a rock thrown from the group smashes a window beside him, the broken glass flying past him. A couple of pieces cut him. He stands there perspiring, rumpled, blood running down from a cut on the cheek. His wife breaks away from the group to throw herself into his arms. He buries his face against her. We can see the crowd converging on the porch.)

VOICE ONE: It must have been him.

VOICE TWO: He's the one.

VOICE THREE: We got to get Charlie. *(Another rock lands on the porch. Charlie pushes his wife behind him, facing the group.)*

CHARLIE: Look, look I swear to you . . . it isn't me . . . but I do know who it is . . . I swear to you . . . I do know who it is. I know who the monster is here. I know who it is that doesn't belong. I swear to you I know.

DON *(pushing his way to the front of the crowd):* All right, Charlie, let's hear it!

(Charlie's eyes dart around wildly.)

CHARLIE: It's . . . it's . . .

MAN TWO *(screaming):* Go ahead, Charlie, tell us.

CHARLIE: It's . . . it's the kid. It's Tommy. He's the one!

(There's a gasp from the crowd as we see Sally holding the boy. Tommy at first doesn't understand and then, realizing the eyes are all on him, buries his face against his mother.)

SALLY *(backs away):* That's crazy! He's only a boy.

WOMAN ONE: But he knew! He was the only one who knew! He told us all

about it. Well, how did he know? How *could* he have known?
(Various people take this up and repeat the question.)
VOICE ONE: How could he know?
VOICE TWO: Who told him?
VOICE THREE: Make the kid answer.
(The crowd starts to converge around the mother who grabs Tommy and starts to run with him. The crowd starts to follow, at first walking fast, and then running after him.

Suddenly Charlie's lights go off and the lights in other houses go on, then off.)
MAN ONE *(shouting):* It isn't the kid . . . it's Bob Weaver's house.
WOMAN ONE: It isn't Bob Weaver's house, it's Don Martin's place.
CHARLIE: I tell you it's the kid.
DON: It's Charlie. He's the one.
(People shout, accuse, and scream as the lights go on and off. Then, slowly, in the middle of this nightmarish confusion of sight and sound the CAMERA STARTS TO PULL AWAY until once again we have reached the opening shot looking at the Maple Street sign from high above.)

SCENE 2. *(THE CAMERA CONTINUES TO MOVE AWAY WHILE GRADUALLY BRINGING INTO FOCUS a field. We see the metal side of a space craft which sits shrouded in darkness. An open door throws out a beam of light from the illuminated interior. Two figures appear, silhouetted against the bright lights. We get only a vague feeling of form.)*
FIGURE ONE: Understand the procedure now? Just stop a few of their machines and radios and telephones and lawn mowers . . . throw them into darkness for a few hours, and then just sit back and watch the pattern.
FIGURE TWO: And this pattern is always the same?
FIGURE ONE: With few variations. They pick the most dangerous enemy they can find . . . and it's themselves. And all we need do is sit back . . . and watch.
FIGURE TWO: Then I take it this place . . . this Maple Street . . . is not unique.
FIGURE ONE *(shaking his head):* By no means. Their world is full of Maple Streets. And we'll go from one to the other and let them destroy themselves. One to the other . . . one to the other . . . one to the other—

SCENE 3. *(THE CAMERA PANS UP for a shot of the starry sky, and over this we hear the Narrator's voice.)*
NARRATOR: The tools of conquest do not necessarily come with bombs and explosions and fall-out. There are weapons that are simply thoughts, attitudes, prejudices—to be found only in the minds of men. For the record, prejudices can kill and suspicion can destroy and a thoughtless, frightened search for a scapegoat has a fall-out all its own for the children . . . and the children yet unborn. *(A pause)* And the pity of it is . . . that these things cannot be confined to . . . The Twilight Zone!

(FADE TO BLACK.)

THE END

A Sample TV Script

EVANSTON HIGHLIGHTS*

TV PRODUCTION CLASS SCRIPT (Evanston, Illinois, Township High School)

VIDEO	AUDIO
WS OF SET	1. MUSIC: THEME: FADE UP AND UNDER
CU SUPER ''Evanston Highlights''	2. ANNCR:
	3. ''Evanston Highlights:''. . . . Each week at this
	4. time, Evanston Township High School presents for
	5. your viewing pleasure. . . . the best in teenage
LOSE SUPER	6. talent . . .And now . . . here is our master of
	7. ceremonies—David Cohen.
(M.C. COHEN WALKS INTO SET)	8. MUSIC: FADE THEME UP AND OUT
DOLLY IN TO MS OF M.C. COHEN	9. M.C. COHEN:
	10. Hello. . . . I'm glad to have you with us
	11. again. As you know. . . . we on ''Evanston
CU OF COHEN	12. Highlights,'' try to bring you what we feel

*Ordinarily each new sequence of numbers beginning with 1 would indicate the start of a new page. For the purpose of this book, we have disgarded this practice.

13. are the highlights of Evanston Township

14. High School. . . . the students whose names

15. will someday be spelled out in dazzling

16. lights for everyone to see. . . . .

MS OF COHEN & SET   17. As you can see, we try to highlight the

18. important thing. . . . our talent . . . by

19. keeping our sets, lights, and programs

20. as simple as possible. The talent, the

21. creativity, and the imagination of these

22. young classmates of ours are the important

23. things to us. And. . . . by focusing your

24. attention on them alone. . . . we hope that you

25. will understand why we feel this way. . . . .

1. Our pace is slow and easy. . . . because we

VIDEO   AUDIO

2. want you to sit back and relax and know

3. that this is one program that is meant for

4. your enjoyment. . . . . The show we have for you

5. today is really something special. . . . it's

6. a blend of the rare and the popular. . . . .

7. I think you'll see what I mean in a few

MS OF COHEN   8. minutes. . . . . Rather than tell you, I'd like

9. to introduce you to our first guest. . . . a

10. young lady who is only in her first year

11. at ETHS and has already gained the respect

12. and admiration of everyone. . . . a truly

MS OF DIANE WALKING
   INTO SET   13. artistic performer. . . . Diane Haller.

14. WELCOME AND INTERVIEW:

CU OF DIANE   15. a) Diane, how long have you been

16.   studying?

17. b) Do you get much time to practice

        along with all your studying?

	19. c) Are there any school activities
	20. that give you an opportunity to
	21. dance?
	22. d) Have you ever made any professional
	23. appearances?
	24. e) Do you plan to make this a career?
	25. f) What is the number you're going to
	26. do for us today?
DOLLY BACK TO MS AS COHEN LEAVES	1. M.C. COHEN
	2. (INTRODUCES DANCER AND LEAVES SET.)
MS OF DIANE	3. MUSIC:
CU OF DIANE	4. DANCE

VIDEO	AUDIO
MS OF DIANE	5. DANCE
FADE TO BLACK	6. MUSIC: FADE OUT
FADE UP ON MS OF M.C. COHEN	7. That was Diane Haller . . . a truly artistic
	8. dancer . . . something that high school students don't
	9. get a chance to see very often. . . . . . .
CU OF M.C. COHEN	10. But . . . if you remember . . . we promised you
	11. something on the popular side too. I'm sure
	12. that you're all going to enjoy this next act
	13. . . . . . it's a group of Evanston students who
MWS OF SET AS GROUP ENTERS	14. call themselves ''The Aches and Pains.''
DOLLY IN TO MS OF M.C. COHEN AND SINGERS	15. M.C. COHEN INTRODUCES DAN PAYNE WHO THEN
CU OF EACH AS INTRODUCED	16. INTRODUCES THE MEMBERS OF THE GROUP
MS OF M.C. COHEN & GROUP	17. INTERVIEW:
CU OF PERSON ANSWERING	18. a) How did your group get started?
MS OF GROUP	19. b) Before the show, you mentioned that

	20. you had written the number you are
	21. going to do for us today. . . .How did
	22. you get started composing songs?
	23. c) How long do you have to practice
	24. to get a number worked up?
	1. d) What are your future plans for ''The
	2. Aches and Pains''?
DOLLY BACK TO MWS AS M.S. COHEN LEAVES	3. M.C. COHEN:
	4. (Introduces group and leaves set.)
MS GROUP	5. SONG
CU PIANO PLAYER	6. SONG

VIDEO	AUDIO
MS OF GROUP	7. SONG
MS OF PIANO PLAYER & GROUP	8. SONG
CU OF SPEAKER	9. SONG
MS OF GROUP	10. SONG
FADE TO BLACK	11. SONG ENDS
FADE UP ON MS OF M.C. COHEN	12. M.C. COHEN:
	13. I'd like to thank you for being with us
	14. today. . . . and I hope you've enjoyed our
	15. show. . . . . Tune in again next Wednesday at
	16. this same time . . . as we bring some more
DOLLY OUT TO MWS OF M.C. COHEN AND SET	17. talented students out of the shadows. . . .
	18. and into. . . . the ''Evanston Highlights.''
	19. (M.C. STEPS BACK AND BEGINS TALKING TO
	20. TALENT WHO ARE WALKING ON TO SET.)
	21. MUSIC: THEME UP AND UNDER
SUPER: TITLE CARD	22. ANNCR:
	23. This has been . . . ''Evanston Highlights'' . . .

LOSE SUPER	24. with your M.C. David Cohen . . . Produced and
SUPER PROD. CREDITS	25. directed by the ever-growing and ever-better,
LOSE SUPER SUPER: E.T.H.S.	1. TV Club of . . . Evanston Township High School.
	2. Remember . . . Don't just guess . . . Tune in to
	3. E.T.H.S.
LOSE SUPER	4. MUSIC: THEME UP AND THEN FADED OUT
FADE TO BLACK	

7

Taping the Message

In April 1956, representatives of the National Association of Radio and Television Broadcasters, meeting in Chicago, Ill., witnessed the demonstration of a machine that was to have as great an impact on the communications field as the printing press had centuries ago; a machine that could record and store visual images so they could be played back and viewed again.

Previous to this time there were two methods of recording television pictures, both unsatisfactory; the kinescope recording and the disc recording. The kinescope recording was a movie made of the pictures from the television receiver tube, or kinescope. Its quality was unpredictable because it had to go through so many different stages and forms, and was never very good. The disc recording was unmanageable because of its size. It required a disc forty-two inches in diameter to record less than 30 minutes of sound and picture. After April 1956, however, live television and film moved back into second place in favor of this new form of recording—videotape.

The videotape recorder looks like a large-size audio tape recorder, with which you are probably familiar. The camera and microphone are plugged into the recorder with its reel of magnetic recording tape. The electronic impulses of television pictures and sound are recorded on this special magnetic videotape, which can be played back later. At that time, the impulses are again converted to picture and sound for viewing on the television screen. The newer and smaller video cassette recorders allow the freedom only enjoyed by super 8 film cameras a few years ago.

Advantages of Videotape

As a kind of middle ground between live television and film, the videotape recording has many advantages.

1. It makes possible delayed broadcasts for the various time zones in the United States.
2. It makes possible more convenient scheduling of programs and facilities.
3. It enables television programmers to use all kinds of equipment, supplies, and materials that cannot be transported into the studio.
4. It provides for more efficient use of staff, time, and equipment.
5. It permits the scheduling of intermission time—not always possible with live television.
6. It provides opportunity for editing and updating material.
7. It produces a filmed picture that looks like live television.
8. It relieves the staff of the pressure involved in live production.
9. It can be played back immediately.
10. It can be erased and used again.
11. It allows television productions to be taped on locations outside the television studio.

Delayed broadcasts. Before videotape was available, evening telecasts originating in New York either had to be aired earlier in the midwest or the west (usually in a poorer time slot), or repeated at additional cost, or filmed on inferior quality kinescope for later playback. Now, a newscast can be recorded on videotape in New York and played back at 6:00 P.M. in each of the time zones. Guest performers who don't wish to get up early for the *Today* show or *Good Morning, America,* both at 7:00 A.M., can be videotaped the night before. The internationally famous scientist who will be out of town on the night of an ecology special can be interviewed and recorded in the studio before he or she leaves and the videotape used on the program. Programs for weekends and holidays can be videotaped in advance, making it possible for the staff to work five days a week and broadcast a complete seven-day schedule of programs.

More convenient scheduling. It is certainly more convenient to re-do a show, when necessary, while the studio is set up, while the crew is there, while instructions are fresh in everyone's mind, and while the cast is still together in the studio. The immediate playback of a videotape recording of a show permits directors to see immediately if they have a good "take" before dismissing the cast and crew. The time-consuming process of developing and printing a filmed program is eliminated. With videotape, a playback is possible as soon as the tape can be rewound.

Remote materials. It is also more convenient to take a camera and videotape recorder to a museum and videotape a large exhibit than to bring the exhibit to the studio, even if permission were granted to do so. Certain objects are so huge that they must be videotaped on the spot and the tape inserted into the program. Imagine trying to bring a dinosaur skeleton or a piece of farm machinery into your studio!

Efficiency. It is often more efficient to videotape parts of a show at odd hours, when there are fewer demands on studio and staff. If the studio has only six scoop lights and the programs require four in one scene and three in another, it is more efficient to shoot one of those scenes at another time and have it ready on videotape than to change lights from one side of the studio to another in the middle of a show.

In commercials, the sponsor often wants the M.C. or the star of the show to give a plug for the product. The talent can do a better job on both the commercial and the show itself if he or she

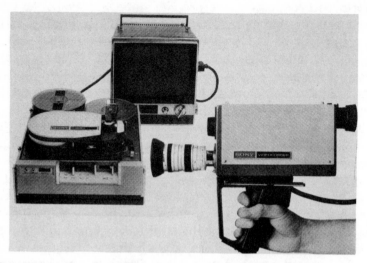

This very compact and very portable unit consists of a camera, recorder, and playback unit. It uses one-half inch black and white tape.

can videotape the commercial separately and concentrate on the show alone while it is being recorded. (If segments like this are taped at different times, be sure the talent is wearing the same costume. Students' costumes can be hung in their lockers for several days.)

Another efficient shortcut is to videotape standard opening and closing sequences for a television series. These can be played back for each show, rather than photographing them live. Some directors use a videotape of the background and then super new title cards for each show. Notice the open and close of many of the popular network television programs you watch. They are all on tape, ready to be inserted each week with new titles and credits supered over the same background.

Intermission time.   Live television does not allow for an intermission, as does the theater or the time-out of a sports event. Air time moves ahead with no breaks for changing scenery, adjusting make-up, rearranging properties, or changing costumes. Videotaping makes it possible to present one segment of the program, provide a break, then tape another segment. When played back on the air, the two segments appear to be continuous.

Editing and updating.   One of the most advantageous features of videotape is the fact that it can be edited and updated. Since a good videotape can be replayed a hundred times without noticeable deterioration, it is important that facts and statements that need to be altered for later use can be easily corrected by editing. The reusability of the tape is an important financial consideration. Since it can be erased and used again and again, updating the content becomes practicable as well as possible.

For instance, a television series on science taped during the summer is made ready for fall playback by editing a reference to cancer research so that it includes the latest developments. Likewise, a discussion of women's rights could easily and appropriately be replayed months later except for the statements regarding ratification of the Equal Rights Amendment. If the two minutes devoted to the status of the amendment could be edited after ratification, the entire tape would be suitable for replay.

Videotape looks like live television.   On the home television screen, it is impossible to distinguish between a videotape playback and a live show. Therefore, a director can mix live material with taped material for greater variety and flexibility, and it will all look the same to the home viewer. Special effects, so desirable in commercials and drama, can be achieved by combining taped backgrounds and sets with live performers. A ballet dancer—live—can be supered over a box of soap powder on tape. A trampoline artist can appear to be bouncing off a record turntable. Tape makes possible a variety of such combinations.

Relief from pressure.   Perhaps the most important advantage in taping a program—at least as far as the beginner is concerned—is the release from the one-time-this-is-it pressure. You can be more relaxed when you know that if you make a minor mistake, the flub can be edited out of the tape. If you make a major error, you can retape the entire segment or even the entire program.

Some directors choose to tape a dress rehearsal and play it back immediately for cast and crew. If it is as good a show as the director thinks can be obtained, then cast and crew can be dismissed, saving hours of valuable time. If the rehearsal reveals weak spots or mistakes, they can be discussed before the actual show, which may be live or taped. Suppose the final production of a school television program is to take place after school. Sometime during the school day, the show can be rehearsed and recorded for playback. During the playback, the director may suggest that two students change positions so that one is nearer the mike, or that the trumpet be sprayed with anti-shine, or that one girl take off her sparkling earrings.

Immediate playback.   The value of the "instant replay" to the sports fan is well known. When a videotape recorder is used for instructional purposes, the value of immediate playback is equally impressive. A football coach takes a small videotape recorder to the football field during August scrimmage sessions and videotapes each play. Immediately, the squad gathers around the monitor to watch the replay while the coach points out what is wrong, where the line is not opening the holes, where the backfield missed an opening, and where the pass defense was weak. If the coach had to wait for the film to be developed and processed before showing the squad how they ran the play, many of them would have forgotten what happened.

Erasures.   Like audio tape, videotape can be erased—either the entire tape or a small portion. Erasing and redoing part of the tape saves time; erasing all the tape and reusing it saves money.

Newer and smaller video cassette recorders allow the studio to go practically anywhere.

Kinds of Videotape Recorders

Because of their obvious advantages, the videotape recorders have become an essential part of a well-equipped television set-up, rather than a luxury. There are many kinds, in both color and black-and-white, with a wide range of prices. The two major categories are *quadruplex* and *helical scan*, the terms referring to the technical process of recording the image on the tape. The quadruplex, which costs around $50,000, records on two-inch tape. This is the professional-broadcast type of equipment used by commercial stations, by most public or educational stations, and by some school and college stations. Many schools and colleges, however, that cannot afford the more expensive models, have achieved satisfactory results with helical scan models using one-inch, half-inch, and even quarter-inch tape. The cheaper models in the $500–$1,000 range now include such features as an electronic editor and an audio dubber, which makes it possible to record without erasing the video signal. A catalogue such as the *Educational/Instructional Broadcasting Buyers Guide* lists companies manufacturing the various types of videotape recorders.

Operation

The operation of a videotape recorder is similar to the procedure for recording audio tape. The tape is threaded from the supply reel, past the recording head or heads (depending upon the model of recorder), and fastened to the take-up reel. On some models, the reels are mounted in a vertical plane; others are horizontal. *Follow precisely the directions given by the manufacturer in the manual of instructions.* If the tape is improperly threaded, the recording will not be satisfactory; in fact, it may be blank.

Most models have five operating buttons or levers: *record*, *stop*, *rewind*, *fast forward*, and *play*. Some have a fast rewind button. Some models record when you push down the record button. Others require that the record button and the play button be pressed down simultaneously in order to record. Again, it is most important to *follow precisely* the manufacturer's directions for recording, rewinding, playback, and erasing.

Suggestions for recording. Regardless of the type of recorder used, the following suggestions will prove helpful sup-

A videotape recorder is operated very similarly to an audio tape. Simply, the tape is threaded from the supply reel, past the recording head or heads, and fastened to the take-up reel.

This unit requires that the record and play buttons be engaged simultaneously, whereas others do not. Because of these subtle differences, it is important that the manual of instructions, as well as any suggestions, be fastened securely to the lid of the recorder.

Though most recorders are similar in operation, it is important to follow precisely the manufacture's directions for recording, rewinding, playback, and erasing.

plements to the manual of instructions, which should always be fastened securely to the lid of the recorder.

1. Be sure the recording head itself is kept free of dust. At least once a week, use the cleaning fluid recommended by the manufacturer. (*Do not* use other cleaning fluids.) Minute particles of dust can result in "drop-outs," those imperfections that appear as white flashes on the television screen.

2. Keep the tape and the recorder in a cool place. Remember that videotape, like audio tape, is affected by heat. The videotape consists of a layer of iron oxide dispersion one-sixth the thickness of a human hair, coated on a plastic backing. Heat causes the plastic backing to stretch and distort the dispersion of iron oxide, resulting in imperfections in picture and sound. If you are using a video cassette, it is important not to touch the tape inside.

3. Be sure to have enough tape on hand before the recording begins. The most commonly used lengths of tape are one-hour and one-half-hour. Some of the newer home recorders have tapes that last up to six hours of recording time.

4. Identify each tape. Label the tape, the reel, and the box in which it is stored. The first shot the camera takes should be a close-up of the identification slate, giving date, time, title, series, director, producer, and technical staff. If the label peels off the reel, or if the reel gets placed in the wrong box, this "slate" identification on the first few inches of the tape will make sure you have accurate information about the show. Don't rely on someone's memory; that person may graduate, or take another job, or even forget.

5. Most videotape recorders have a counter with three or four digits. If the segments are to be taped on one reel, record on the cover box or on a separate sheet of paper the exact location on the tape where each segment can be readily located. For example:

    000–017—Pizza commercial
    017–210—*Mary Poppins*
    210–271—*The Cat and the Canary*
    271–307—Interview with Muhammad Ali

Each time you thread the tape through the recording head and wind it around the reel, the amount of tape you use will vary an inch or two. Even with that slight variation, however, it will be much easier to locate Muhammad Ali between 265 and 275 than to play a dozen snatches here and there before the interview can be located. Be sure to set the counter at 000 before recording and again before playback.

6.   Catalogue the tapes in the same way books are catalogued. Be sure to enter the information in two places; on the box containing the tape and on a card in a file box. The tape-box information can be recorded in pencil. Then it can easily be corrected if the tape is to be erased soon and a new program recorded on it. Because penciled handwriting is easily blurred, many people prefer to use typed labels, which are pasted on the outside of the tape box and can easily be updated by covering them with new labels. The card file of information about each tape is easier to go through than shelves of tapes. If you are going to have a large supply of tapes, work out some system for numbering them. The library uses the Dewey decimal or Library of Congress system based on the subject area. For instance, in the Dewey decimal system, English literature would be 800–899; sports and entertainment would be 700–799; science, 500–599; and history, 900–999. Some people prefer to catalogue the tapes according to the date when they were made. Regardless of the method, *be sure to record the number on the card in the file and on the box containing the tape.*

7.   Be consistent in your method of filing information about the tapes. Most tapes will be requested either by subject or by title. Someone will ask for "the tape we did on misuse of drugs" or "that interview we had with Dr. Kwan." Therefore, cards and tapes should be filed by subject. You can prepare a kind of cross reference, with color coding, by pasting various colored dots (available at any stationery store) on the box of tape and on the file card, to indicate director-producer or any other information needed. In some schools, the most important information is the name of the professor or teacher giving the lecture. If requests for tapes are usually worded, "Dr. Goldberg's lecture," then catalogue the tape under this name.

8.   In the control-room log, keep a complete record of each recording and playback fed over the air or cable, hour-by-

Date	Time	Title	Activity	Staff	Remarks
Mon 2/26	7:30 AM — 8:10 AM	*Combined Studies* rehearsal - Mr. Hanebuth	VTR and playback	E - Smith A - Jones PD - Brown	Only cameramen needed
Mon.	8:30 AM	"Hemingway's Last Work" VTR 808	Playback Feed to 313	E - Smith	Return tape to public library
Mon.	9:00 AM — 10:00 AM	"Twelve Days of Christmas" Dr. Rosewall	Rehearse and tape	E - Smith A - Jones PD - Brown	12 chairs needed for observers

Keeping an hour-by-hour log is a requirement for a commercial station, a necessity for a public broadcasting station, and a time- saver in a school or college situation.

hour through the day and week. This procedure is a legal requirement of a commercial station, a necessity for a public broadcasting station, and a time-saver in a school or college set-up. The log should include the names of the producer and director and of the control-room staff, such as the engineer and audio technician. A commercial station must include every spot, even a thirty-second commercial, but most schools and closed-circuit facilities will find a simplified log of the type shown above quite adequate.

9. Note on each tape the length of time it takes, and be sure to *write down the length of time of each recording*! It may not seem important when you are making the tape recording, but months and even years later, it may be necessary to know whether a certain discussion lasted 45 minutes, 50 minutes, or 59:50. Then someone will have to spend 45 or 50 minutes or an hour timing the tape *unless* the time was recorded easily with five strokes of a pen when the tape was completed.

10. Have a schedule, and plan to weed out regularly any tapes that are no longer usable. Both content and technical quality should be evaluated. If you keep a record of each time a tape is played, either on the tape box or in the control-room log, you will find it easier to judge when it has passed its maximum quality. While weeding out the tapes, take a little time for self-criticism. If tape #100 is no better than tape #2,

something is wrong. If tapes #60 through #90 follow the same format and pattern, someone is in a rut. If tapes #3 through #76 show that same wilted palm tree and the same brocaded chair, it's time for a change. You don't want a returning alumnus to watch a videotape playback and say, "Yes, that tape was made in our studio. I recognize the smear of paint on the draw curtains."

11. If you are using a cassette (either 3.4 U-Beta-VHS), index the counter to locate the precise program on the tape and note the index number for the beginning of the program or sequence wanted.

Editing Videotape

A successful television program demands artistic judgment, imaginative directing, and technical skill, but a basic element in its success is the editing of the tape.

In commercial motion pictures, the film editor's talent can make or break the final product, even though it may leave an actor's dreams on the cutting room floor. Videotape cannot be edited like film because the actual pictures are not visible on the surface of the tape, but it can be edited according to its own properties.

Bob Hope's televised programs of Christmas shows presented to men in the armed services all over the world have become classic examples of how hundreds of hours of performances can be condensed into one hour of tape. They emphasize reaction shots of hundreds of service personnel for the benefit of home viewers, including families watching for a 5-second close-up of a loved one.

The director of a high school production of *The Mikado* and the videotape editor of a local CBS outlet edited a three-hour tape of the musical and cut it to one hour without distorting the sequence of scenes or the plot.

The tape editor and the engineer in a Denver, Colorado, studio made 375 cuts and splices in eight hours of recorded events of the national Boy Scout Jamboree to produce a 60-minute telecast.

The actual process of editing is highly technical and varies according to the type of recorder used. If the director knows that the tape is to be edited, he or she can direct with that fact in mind in order to provide places on the tape where it will be easy to cut and splice. For instance, a scene can be ended with the performers leaving the stage or walking out of the picture frame. The next scene can begin with the performers reentering. The splice can be made at the spot where the stage is empty, with no movement being recorded.

The editor cannot see the images on the surface of the videotape. Therefore, to determine exactly where he or she can cut, the editor must be guided by the magnetized impulses recorded on the tape. Three signals are recorded on it; the picture, the sound, and control track impulses, consisting of quarter-inch spaced blips.

The control track allows videotapes recorded on another machine to be played back on your machine. The control track is similar to the sprocket holes in a film in that it insures the tape is going across the recording and playback heads at an exact speed and location. The control track is usually located on the bottom of the audio recording head. The tracking pulses are not seen in the program but are necessary for proper playback. Most video recorders have a tracking control that can be moved to insure the best picture during playback.

Unlike audio tape, videotape editing is seldom done by physically cutting the tape. In earlier days, the videotape editor did cut the tape, editing as one would edit a film. Today, editing

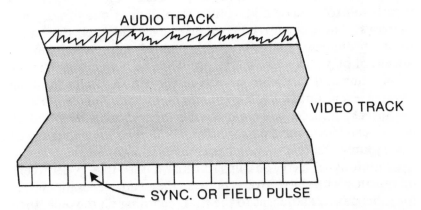

AUDIO TRACK

VIDEO TRACK

SYNC. OR FIELD PULSE

The videotape editor must be guided by the magnetized impulses recorded on the tape. Three signals are recorded: The picture, the sound, and field pulses consisting of quarter-inch spaced blips.

is an electronic process whereby the tape is *dubbed* onto a second tape by the use of an electronic editor. Two machines are needed to edit a tape. The original tape is recorded into proper sequence onto the final tape. New electronic editors can allow a person to see precisely where the edit will take place and will allow the editor to preview and rehearse before attempting to make the final edit on tape. News crews utilize editors to put together clips of tape into a final story to be used in the newscast.

Uses of Videotape

As you improve your taping skills, the uses of videotape will increase in number and variety. They are as numerous as the kinds of machines available and as varied as the creativity of the directors and the technical skill of the operators. For example, because the playback of a videotape enables both the performers and the production staff to see themselves as others see them, a most important use of videotaping is constructive self-criticism. In the mind of performers are visions of what they want to convey to their audience, visions sometimes so vivid and clear to themselves they think they have transmitted it to the cameras. Only when they actually see what comes across can they determine whether or not they communicated (at least as far as the camera is concerned) effectively.

Voice. A voice student who was unable to grasp just what his teacher meant by "improper phrasing" and "an error in breath control" made a videotape recording of one of his vocal exercises. The close-up shots of his head and neck (he had a rather prominent Adam's apple) enabled him, after viewing dozens of playbacks, to observe just when he took a breath at the wrong time and just when he gulped for breath after a too-long phrase—even though the movements were barely perceptible.

Speech. Speech students having difficulties with *s* and *sh* sounds can videotape a passage (five minutes or so) with many of these sounds. During the playback, they can see what they are doing with tongue, teeth, and lips to cause the trouble. After weeks of practice with corrective exercises, they can videotape-record the same passage adjacent to the first recording on the tape, then playback the two segments. In this way, they can assess their improvement and determine what remains to be done.

Done well, video playback is enormously helpful in improving skills. While it is clear that this technique has application in athletics, for example, it can also be used in areas such as speech correction, as shown above. Here, a close-up of the face can dramatically record whether a student is making a "th" sound correctly. Videotapes provide a valuable source of information and should become a library for reference.

Swimming. A swimming coach found it helpful to video-tape through the underwater observation windows in the pool. The playbacks showed the swimmers certain flaws in their techniques that neither their coach nor other members of the swimming team could demonstrate. Above-water taping of a synchronized swimming pattern made it possible for the swimmers to watch the figures they were creating and see where they were out of place.

Basketball. An otherwise excellent basketball player kept missing a high percentage of free throws. So one day, he stood at the free-throw line and shot fouls for half an hour while a camera operator on the out-of-bounds line shot him from every angle in the front, then from both sides and the rear, while a technician recorded on videotape exactly how he performed. The playback of this videotape enabled the player to see how a peculiar out-swing of his left leg was throwing him off center for each shot at the basket. The mannerism was not difficult to correct, once the player could actually see what he was doing.

Production techniques. Performers are not the only ones who profit from the self-criticism made possible by the videotape recorder. The subtleties of production techniques are more readily observed when the staff, free of the pressure of getting the show on the air, can sit down together and discuss what they see and hear being communicated in a show they have just completed. Some directors like to play the tape back twice, once for an evaluation and general impression of the entire show and once for specific criticism of camera work, lighting, audio, transitions, graphics, and so on.

Auditions. Many television directors and some theater directors believe that auditions can be more efficiently handled if the performers are videotaped. The casting director, instead of being overwhelmed by seventy-two renditions of "People" at one sitting, can listen to a few at a time on videotape and replay any of them at his or her leisure.

Tape library. Videotapes provide a valuable record of events. The tapes can be stored, under proper conditions, and become a library for reference. Such a library can also be of assistance during an emergency. If the lights burn out in the studio, if the camera blows up, if the talent breaks a leg, an old tape can be hauled out of the library and the show will go on!

Properly stored, videotapes can become an indispensable reference library, as well as an invaluable aid in emergencies, when lights burn out, the camera blows, etc.

Playbacks can effectively reinforce the historical significance of today's events. When Presidents Eisenhower, Truman, Kennedy, and Johnson died, the televised tributes to these men included playbacks of newscasts and interviews made during their term of office. Many young people were able to observe for themselves the personalities of men who, up to then, had come to life only in their parents' conversation.

In addition to networks and broadcasting stations, various organizations have videotape libraries. The Public Broadcasting Service maintains a library of videotapes that circulate among the educational television stations or are fed to them over telephone lines. There are television libraries, like the Great Plains National Instructional Television Library at Lincoln, Nebraska, which rents and sells videotaped series and programs to educational stations, universities, and schools. The Public Television Library rents videotapes to schools from the television programs seen on the Public Broadcasting System.

At the local level, universities and a few public schools maintain libraries of videotaped lesson and reference materials, programs, and supplementary materials. These are placed in a dial-access information-retrieval system. When someone dials the

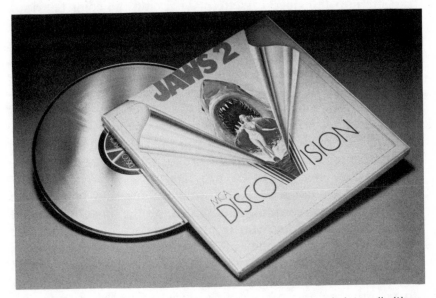

With the advent of the videotape cassette, television expands into a limitless new dimension.

number of a taped lesson or program, the system feeds it into the television receiver in a library carrel.

Videotape's Miracles

Considering the fantastic jobs that can not be performed with videotape recorders, it is no wonder that new uses for videotapes are being developed daily. The tape can now be encased in a cartridge or cassette for recording and/or playback with no threading or handling. In fact, the tape does not leave the cartridge. You can now purchase or rent a video playback for your regular black-and-white or color television set. It is a simple matter to insert a video cassette and play back a program on your television set in the same way your audio cassette player puts music through your stereo. Video cassettes of television programs have been packaged for sale or rental. Now even local libraries are checking out movies for home use on video cassettes just as they check out books. Extensive libraries of these programs are now available, including entire series of courses originally shown on educational television stations. The local dentist can insert a cassette into the video cassette playback on the color television set in the office and show you in living color how the braces will be put on your teeth or how a partial denture is made.

Some companies even rent the playback equipment that you can attach to your receiver. Plug the cassette playback into the antenna outlet of a conventional color or black-and-white television set. Switch to Channel 3 or 4, whichever is open in your locale. Insert a video cassette into the player and depress the play button. The program will appear on the television screen. You can reverse, play back part of the program a second time, or fast-forward to a later part of the program.

Now, with home recorders you can insert a blank video cassette into your recording equipment, set the timer, and go out for the evening. When you return, the television program you missed while you were out will be recorded on a video cassette ready for you to play back whenever you wish. As mentioned in an earlier chapter, many homes are using video cassette recorders to record programs off the air, as well as to create their own television programs with low cost cameras. Television, which long has been limited by what was being broadcast by networks, is undergoing a revolution with new technology such as videotape, cable, and video discs.

Television, which long ago erased the space barriers, permitting us to look into the far corners of the earth and the moon, has now erased the time barrier with the videotape recorder.

Take Two

1. Either as individuals or in small groups, research material on live television. Many of the personalities involved then are still active in the field today. Discuss your findings with your classmates. Assess the differences between live and taped television.

2. Compare and contrast film and videotape.

3. Instant replays have improved arm-chair spectating. Debate whether referees on the field or court should have immediate playback.

VIDEOLAB

1. Develop and implement a catalogue system for your tape library. If you decide to catalogue your tapes by subject, use either the Dewey decimal or Library of Congress system.

   000 General Works
   100 Philosophy
   200 Religion
   300 Social Sciences
   400 Language
   500 Pure Science
   600 Useful Arts
   700 Fine Arts
   800 Literature
   900 History, Travel, Biography

8

Considering Careers in Television

"How can I get on television?" you ask. People get "on" television because they *know* something, *can do* or *have done* something, or *are* somebody. If you have won seven gold medals in the Olympics, you have done something and will have no trouble getting on television. If you are the first woman astronaut, you will find the television networks more than willing to turn their cameras on you, even in your home. If you witnessed the collapse of a section of bleachers during the state basketball tournament, you know something about which television interviewers will want to question you.

Or perhaps your question is worded a bit differently, "How can I get into television?" The *how* cannot be answered until you know the *where*—in what area, through which door, in which specific field. Are you interested in the visually artistic aspects of television? Do you want to produce and direct programs? Do you crave the excitement of on-the-scene reporting of news? Would you like to write feature stories about television performers, or news releases about programs? Would you like to be involved in the business or financial department of television? Would you like to engage in research on program audiences, viewers' acceptance of products and messages, and projections of future plans? Would you like to give the daily weather report? If you can answer *yes* to any of these questions, consider (in alphabetical order) just a few of the doorways through which you might enter television.

Advertising

There are probably more television producer-directors working for advertising agencies than for television stations. In agencies, the television specialists will package, or prepare, a program, getting it ready for the network to present—an advantage for the advertiser who knows what he or she is getting for his or her money because he or she sees the completed program. Agencies use writers, talent, producer-directors, and all types of television personnel who would be involved in the preparation of a program. "Idea people" who can create programs and conceive new ideas for the televised promotion of products are welcomed by agencies, which often have a television department separate from the print-media advertising departments.

Art

If you are interested and talented in commercial art, the graphics department of a television production center may offer you an opportunity. You may prepare title cards or you may letter names, quotations, mottos, and signs. You may draw free-hand hearts and flowers to decorate posters. You may design posters to illustrate an idea. For instance, one graphic artist was given the assignment of creating a poster to illustrate the advantages of using visual aids. He drew a cartoon picturing a startled corpse rising from a casket with the caption: "Let media put life into your presentation."

Larger studios need personnel qualified in scenic design and set production. In such a position you would perform the same kinds of tasks as the technical theater staff of a school or college drama department; designing sets, constructing scenery, and painting sets and stage props. In addition, you would have to meet the lighting and color needs of the television camera and work within the space restrictions of the studio.

Film is a major aspect of television, as indicated by the many schools that train students for careers in this area. The names of such schools usually include the words *film* or *motion pictures* in their titles, such as "radio-film-television" or "television-radio-motion pictures." In some studios, still-photography is handled through the art department; in others, the news or programming staff has the responsibility for all photographic assignments.

Broadcast Journalism

A curriculum in journalistic reporting is supplemented by radio and television techniques. Students who wish to major in broadcast journalism have their choice of many colleges and universities, as well as specialized communication schools.

Business

Finances, sales, accounting, purchasing, budgeting, and personnel are all areas of the business side of television. In the first five of these areas, you would work with the receipts and expenditures involved in television programs. In the personnel division, you would be responsible for employee relationships, the hiring and placement of staff, training programs, and preparing payrolls for the accounting department. In the business of television, you might be responsible for publicity releases on the station's schedule and special new programs. You might work as a marketing specialist, developing sales campaigns and working with the program manager to develop programs that can be sold. You might be a time salesperson, visiting various industries, companies, and organizations to persuade them to buy time on your station's program schedule.

Education

The educational aspects of television may be the door through which you want to enter upon your career, either in a public broadcasting (educational) station or in a commercial station. You might become a specialist in children's programs, or a liaison between the station and the public schools receiving educational programs.

Some stations group educational and religious program responsibilities in a public affairs department. In such a department you would work on the commercial station's broadcasts of Sunday church services, special religious holiday programs, the five-minute devotions when the station signs on the air, on-the-site visits to innovative educational programs, lecture series, interviews with educators, or features such as "How to Fill Out Your Income Tax Form."

You may want to enter television through the teaching field—that is, teach science for an educational station; or teach Spanish for a series on a commercial station with an early morning show for teachers; or teach food preparation for a commercial series sponsored by a large company like General Foods. Industrial arts teachers frequently become involved in television through presenting workshop programs for the do-it-yourself handyman.

The similarities between teaching and broadcasting frequently become apparent to students studying television production. For instance, a high school girl working as a camera operator on a school series became greatly interested in the techniques of picture composition that would make a science project understandable to students of low mental ability—so interested in fact, that she switched her college major from communications to education. The successful television program must capture and retain the attention of the viewer; so must a teacher. The television program must achieve its purpose by making its message clear; so must a teacher. The television program must take into consideration the personality, interest level, past experiences, needs, prejudices, and probable receptivity of the audience; so must a teacher.

The growing numbers of colleges and even high schools with broadcasting facilities, the expansion of closed-circuit television, and the increasing number of public broadcasting stations are

Emmy award-winning anchor team Bill Kurtis and Walter Jacobson of WBBM-TV in Chicago.

providing many opportunities for combining careers in teaching and broadcasting. You might be interested in a teaching job at a university or high school, training students for the broadcasting industry.

Many educational producers are using the video market to aid instruction. Some of the larger producers, including *Agency for Instructional Television* and *Children's Television Workshop*, produce hundreds of television programs for elementary and secondary schools.

A recent issue of the *Newsletter* of the National Association of Educational Broadcasters includes these examples of typical positions available:

Instructor in Radio-TV for midwestern college. New department (2 years old) with color studios. Requires extensive practical experience in production and/or teaching. Able to teach announcing, newswriting, scriptwriting, programming, production, and station management. M.A. required, Ph.D. preferred. Salary $13,500–18,000 for academic year.

Communications Production Supervisor for California college. To supervise production staff and general operation of educational TV studio, playback center, remote truck, microwave system, ITFS and remote productions. Duties include: meeting with faculty to develop effective uses of ETV in instructional programs, training and evaluation of staff, preparing budgets and reports, supervising scheduling of productions. Requires: BA with specialization in communications plus four years of ETV experience, or MA and three years experience. Classroom teaching background desirable. Salary $15,000–$22,000.

Medical Producer-Writer for above facility. Requires minimum of a B.A. degree plus two years experience in medical communications to produce program materials for color CCTV operation in a new medical school and teaching hospital. Duties will include either clinical or instructional activities. Faculty status available. Open immediately.

Engineering

No television station can be more successful than the quality of the signal it transmits. Therefore, the training and efficiency of the technical personnel (and the capabilities of the equipment) are the most essential elements in the station's operation. You may want to function in the design, operation, installation, or maintenance of the station's equipment from studio to transmitter. You may prefer to work in the quiet seclusion of the transmitting station or in the ulcer-producing control room where the action is. You may want to become a consulting engineer who writes specifications and supervises the purchase and installation of equipment for a station in a city, a school system, or a developing foreign country. You may want to become a technical specialist in the operation of videotape machines. The technicians are often required to have an FCC First Class Radio Telephone License. These technicians also operate the new minicam equipment used by news departments.

Law

You may prefer the corporation law aspects of the broadcasting industry, such as interpreting the Federal Communications Commission regulations and the copyright rulings. Reading the law on union contracts can be anything but dull. For instance, one kind of legal problem involved might be the contract for the operator of a "video font." This is the machine that prints letters for those instantaneous television signs used in sports events. (Joe Blow catches a pass for a gain of 35 yards. Immediately we see a sign, supered over Joe running back up the field that announces that his total yardage for four passes in this game is 85.) Is it legal for a secretary-typist to operate this machine, which works like a typewriter, or must the station hire a $300-a-week technician because the machine operates electronically? Or how would you interpret the union contract in the case of a performing horse that has to be brought in an elevator to the third floor studio? Is the horse the responsibility of the stagehands because he is a prop, or of the producer because he is "talent"?

The legal department of a television station must interpret the laws regarding copyrights; the selling or granting of rights to copy the station's programs and play them back; the defense of the station in suits involving breach of contract or censorship of scripts; the preparation of evidence for the station's license renewal by the Federal Communications Commission—in short, the activities of a corporation lawyer.

Library Services

The need for the services of an efficient reference librarian is obvious to anyone who has tried to prepare a documentary, but a librarian is also needed to catalogue scripts and script material as well as to catalogue and file tapes, records, and films. Some studios have a special music librarian.

Management

To be a profitable business, a television station or network must have personnel with management training and skill to plan, execute, and oversee the functions of station management, guest relations, studio scheduling and operation, clerical staff, leasing of telephone and cable lines, and relations with the networks. Station managers may appear to be far removed from the television programs themselves as they operate on a day-by-day basis. However, they need to know the functional problems of every phase of programming, production, sales, cost analysis, and engineering if they are going to supervise the relationships of the departments to each other. More and more they are being charged with the responsibility of becoming responsive to the needs of the community the station serves and must be able to prove that the station operates in the "public interest, convenience, and necessity," as stated in the license allowing use of the public airwaves.

Music

Small stations may have few, if any, live musical programs, but most of them will need the services of a producer-director who knows music, a continuity writer who knows music, a librarian who knows music, an announcer who knows music, technicians who can transmit good tone quality for music, a legal consultant who knows copyright regulations regarding music, and a wealth of varied musical recordings in all categories of musical taste. In one instance, a large university television station faced with the problem of hiring one producer-director from a group of five competent applicants, selected a less experienced applicant solely on the basis of his musical background. Notice how many of your favorite television personalities will say during an interview, "I started out as a disc jockey on a little station out in Podunk."

Programming

This area sounds like an "idea" or "think tank" field, and so it is. However, it also involves policies and, in varying degrees, special events, public affairs, religious programs, sports, films, politics, education, news, and drama. The Radio-Television News Directors Association estimates that more than one-third of the employees of all radio and television stations are involved in the preparation and presentation of news.

The field of production is usually considered as one part of program responsibility, although in a very large production center, the two may be separated just to simplify administration. The directors, camera operators, audio technicians, control-room technicians, graphic artists, floor managers, and lighting technicians are all part of the "production" of a program. Officially, engineers may be listed as belonging to the engineering department, but when they start shading the cameras in the control room during the broadcast of a show, they are part of the production staff. Graphic artists may never enter the studio, but if they have made the title cards and lettered the names of speakers to be supered over their pictures, they are part of the production staff. The make-up artist and the costumer who prepare the performer to make his or her appearance on camera are part of the production staff. Literally, the production staff involves all who directly help with "putting on the show."

The jobs in the production area might include driving a remote-unit truck to a high school to tape a track meet or to Convention Hall in Atlantic City to present the Miss America pageant live. Or your job might include breakfast with an ambassador's wife, to plan an interview with the ambassador. You might have to sit for hours at the doors of a jury room waiting to "cover" the story when the jurors bring their verdict to the judge. Your job might be in an office, where, armed with telephone, card file, persistence, and ingenuity, you assemble for a production a parrot that sings, a red-haired ten-year-old boy who can yodel, a grandfather clock eight feet high, an Edison gramophone, a German howitzer, or the largest pizza ever made. Your job might be to press costumes, empty wastebaskets, and take orders for black coffee and corned beef on rye. You could be the departmental "gopher," so called because you are always being asked to "go for coffee," "go for more ice," or "go for some pencils." Program and production jobs vary from dull routine to continuous chaos.

Religious Broadcasting

If you are interested in religion, in the social interpretation of theology, and in broadcasting, you can combine those interests in a range of religious programming; discussions, drama, music, news, dance, festivals, seasonal and holiday specials—in fact, everything from a liturgical service to Stan Freberg's stylized "go to church" spots. Many of the individual denominations have their own radio and television commissions, and the three major faiths have councils on broadcasting, such as the Broadcasting and Film Commission, the National Catholic Office for Radio and Television, and the Department of Radio and Television of the Jewish Theological Seminary.

Research

The young lady standing on the corner of Main and Capital streets with a clipboard under her arm, asking each passerby, "What kind of breakfast cereal do you prefer? Who are the sponsors of *Sixty Minutes*?" may be employed by the research division of an advertising agency or by a television station. The young man opening mail bags at a local station, who tallies on a wall map the requests for a free booklet as part of a "mail pull" advertising campaign, is working in another facet of research. Your job may be to assemble and interpret statistics or to assemble research data from rating services and network departments and apply them to the station's program evaluation.

Because of the sizable financial investment in program and advertising costs, both the networks and the advertisers need to know how large an audience a certain television program is drawing, and how effectively it is promoting the sale of the advertiser's product. This need for television research has given rise to a number of rating services: A. C. Nielsen, Videodex, TeleQue, Trendex, Pulse, and ARB (American Research Bureau), to name just a few. Some of these companies use mechanical devices fastened to the home receivers of a scientific sample of viewers; some use personal interviews; others use diaries. The A. C. Nielsen Company, for instance, uses an audimeter, placed in the television set of the viewers, which records the times at which the set is on and the channel to which it is tuned. The American Research Bureau uses the diary study, based on forms which a family fills out each day for a week, noting the program being viewed and the number, sex, and age of the viewers. Pulse uses "aided recall," personal interviews in which a list of programs reminds the interviewee of what was available for viewing. One popular method of audience research is the coincidental study, a telephone survey made while the program is being broadcast.

So if you choose to enter the field of television research, you may work with people, with pencil and paper, with telephones, and with computers.

Talent

Your job in television may be in front of the camera, or—to use the industry's expression—"on camera." You may be under contract to a model agency which sends you to the station to make a commercial. You may perform on camera not because you are handsome or beautiful, but because you have a skill, such as Julia Child and her cooking show.

If you want to act on television, you should first become a successful stage actor. Television newscasters begin as journalists; television announcers begin in radio or theater; television singers, musicians, and dancers begin in stage shows, concert halls, and floor shows; and television actors begin as performers in theater or radio productions. For example, Beatrice Arthur, the star of *Maude*, entered television after becoming an established actress on the stage and in the movies.

Producers and directors usually work through talent agencies, which they rely on to send them the talent suited to a program's particular needs. A really good talent agent can make the difference between your "getting the breaks" as an actor and remaining on the unemployed lists.

If you are wondering whether you have the talent to be a successful television performer, if you are wondering what it takes to make the grade, consider the words of Alvina Krause, Northwestern University's famous teacher of so many who have "made the big time". "Talent. What is it? In the final analysis is it not the capacity to work? To work intensively, intelligently and endlessly to master the skills, inner and outer, of his art."

Writing

You probably think of television writers as semi-mad geniuses working in seclusion. True, on occasions they may be lucky enough to write their copy away from the busyness of the studio or production center. More often, however, they have to dash it off one paragraph at a time, while a typist translates the hand-written scrawls into readable script and rushes it off, one page at a time, to the newscast after the show is on the air. A writer may also prepare orderly copy—timed, revised, and submitted without the dramatic flurry usually associated with the news room. He or she may prepare dramatic scripts, adapt other writers' works for television, or write situation comedy dialogue, news documentaries, sports reviews, news releases about performers or programs, feature stories for broadcasting trade journals, study guides for class assignments on television viewing, or the station manager's editorials. As a writer you may work alone or in conference with a team of writers. You may write at home and mail your material to a team of writers you will work it into the routine they are developing for a particular show. Seldom do original TV scripts come to the small screen without many changes.

New Fields

In addition to these more or less familiar categories, new areas are opening all the time in communications and related fields. Who would have thought a few years ago that a television camera operator in Houston, Texas, would be able to pan, tilt, or zoom a television camera located on the moon? Who can imagine the new uses for cameras and tape recorders on space stations? The satellites that transmit television programs to and from most areas of the world are now taken for granted. The *Voice of America*, once limited to radio, is taking on new dimensions in its programs beamed into Communist countries. The video cassette promises to make collections of television programs for playback at home as common as record collections or stereo tapes. Cable television, growing every day, with its local programming requirements and its capability of making television available to remote areas, has added another category to jobs available in the field. The film and television companies now producing television programs for syndicated distribution to stations throughout the nation have proved to be a growing source of employment for television directors, technicians, and talent.

Many performers enter television through the back door. For instance, one student whose college training was in television engineering and whose hobby was art and amateur theatricals, combined the two areas in his job as scene designer for color television programs. A radio actress found her place in television because she could simulate any kind of baby cry on cue. The director of auto-show exhibits with flare and style found advertising agencies in need of his imaginative directorial skill in the packaging of television shows. The director of the radio-television department of a university in the District of Columbia found herself in great demand as a make-up consultant for political figures appearing on television. Roger Ailes, who produced the one-hour shows for Nixon's presidential campaign, started out as a prop boy on the *Mike Douglas Show* and within three years became the producer.

Because many college television facilities operate twelve to fifteen hours a day, they need personnel and studio crews for longer periods of time than can be supplied by students in television production classes. So extra students are hired to operate equipment and to perform odd jobs around the studio. An occasional student who signs up for this work only to earn tuition money discovers that he or she enjoys television production and chooses communications as his or her major field.

Although many persons gain entry into television through conspicuous success in a related medium or in the entertainment field, probably just as many go directly into the industry, beginning at the bottom. When bad weather prevents personnel from reaching the studios, or when the network is faced with a strike by union camera operators, you hear or read that "operations are being staffed by network executives." You may or may not know that Vice-President Ramirez began as a dolly pusher in a small station, that Comptroller Jones began his television career as the audio engineer in a local station, that Sales Manager Yu was once a boom mike operator, and that Research Director Desai once shaded cameras in the control room of a station so small that the five employees had to take turns at every job to keep it on the air. This practical knowledge of the daily functioning of the elements of production is an asset that can be achieved only through actual experience, hard work, and an attitude of dedication and cooperation.

Education for Television Careers

The National Association of Broadcasters, the trade association of the radio and television industry, has expressed its need for a certain type of young people to prepare for careers in radio and television, as follows: "We need young people with the ingenuity, vision and boldness necessary to push television further ahead—to lead it into an ever expanding future of service."

Many high schools, colleges, and universities have major departments in the communications field. The Association for Professional Broadcasting Educators, an organization of two hundred schools and colleges offering substantial course work in

Carolyn Bailey conducted a series of interviews on nutrition for public television station WWVU-TV in Morgantown, West Virginia.

radio and television will supply information about its member schools. Many junior colleges and commercial or trade schools also give courses in broadcasting skills.

The armed services offer training in the technical areas of broadcasting, such as those available through the Signal Corps, and provide experience in the production and direction of television programs. During the 1971 television season, the first year that the U.S. Armed Forces bought time for advertising as part of its voluntary enlistment campaign, they spent more than $3.7 million on television programming.

The competitive nature of the industry gives an advantage to the college-trained employee who has developed broad vision, depth of understanding, and skill in learning new concepts rapidly. Schools that operate their own educational stations can offer the student a realistic laboratory in which to explore interests and to develop skill and understanding. Commercial stations near some colleges may offer internships to students to work while they learn.

In the final analysis, you consider a career in television in two ways: (1) through an introspective analysis of yourself, your ideal way of living, your personal development goals, your attitudes about social responsibility, your ability to work under pressure, your ability to work with people, your flexibility, your philosophy about the place of the media in a democratic society; and (2) through an in-depth study and analysis of the field of television.

Take Two

1. Research the current requirements and salaries for the positions described in this chapter. Discuss with your classmates the advantages and disadvantages of positions in which you have interest.

2. Watch the credit lines following the local news. Notice the variety of people and positions listed. You may even wish to call the local station and inquire about their hiring practices. Would you consider television a viable profession?

VIDEOLAB

1. Invite professionals in the television field to come and speak to your class. Be sure to indicate what areas of the profession you would like them to be prepared to address. Compare the reality of television professions with what you have learned through research.

2. If possible, arrange to visit the local station.

Appendix

Testing 1-2-3

When you say "Testing 1-2-3" into a mike, you are check-ing—for yourself or the audio technician—whether or not the mike is live, whether or not you are coming across, and whether or not the volume is satisfactory. In a similar way, this section will help you check (1) whether or not you have acquired addi-tional knowledge about television, (2) whether or not you have developed skills in television production, and (3) whether or not you now act as a more sensitive, responsible viewer.

A. 1. Define or explain each of these terms as it relates to tele-vision:

a.	*back timing*	f.	*lavaliere*
b.	*clearance*	g.	*dry run*
c.	*scoop*	h.	*frame*
d.	*FCC*	i.	*rack*
e.	*Nielsen*	j.	*boom*

  2. Distinguish between
     a. *truck and tilt*
     b. *image orthicon* and *vidicon*
     c. *script and rundown*
     d. *unidirectional* and *nondirectional*
     e. *teleprompter* and *aspect ratio*

  3. List four sources of information about what to watch on telvision.

  4. What advice can you give a young person who wants to write for television?

B. 1. Thread a reel of tape on your videotape recorder, plug in the camera, the microphone, and the AC line. Record an activity of some of your classmates and play back what you recorded. What kind of written record did you keep of what you did?

2. As a director, what term or terms should you use to instruct a camera operator to:
    a. Move the camera dolly directly to the left   _____
    b. Pan the camera up or down (other than "pan")   _____
    c. Rotate the lens turret to bring a one-inch lens into shooting position   _____
    d. Give a wide-angle shot that would include the entire scene   _____
    e. Follow a speaker who is walking left   _____

3. List the duties of a floor manager.

4. Demonstrate the correct hand signal to communicate each of these instructions:
    a. *Stand by*
    b. *Begin*
    c. *Move toward the mike*
    d. *Look at camera #2*
    e. *Talk faster*
    f. *Wind it up*
    g. *Louder*
    h. *Five minutes left*
    i. *Thirty seconds left*
    j. *Stop*

5. List four duties a camera operator should perform before the show begins.

6. List the duties the camera operator should perform after the show.

7. Serve on a production crew. Find out from the director what you did not do correctly. (You probably won't have to ask.)

8. Identify each of the following parts of the camera by pointing to it and operating it if it is manipulable:
    a. *turret*
    b. *focus*
    c. *viewfinder*
    d. *tally light*
    e. *f-stop adjustment*
    f. *focal length*

9. A television director once said that his job was to "direct people and ideas first, cameras and facilities second." Explain why you agree or disagree with that statement.

C. 1. On what basis do you select television shows for entertainment?

2. With what questions do you now evaluate all kinds of television shows?

3. To what extent are you as an individual responsible for what's available to television viewers?

4. You are an officer of the Young Republocratic Club. Your job is to plan a radio, television, and newspaper campaign for the Republocratic candidate for governor. What would you plan for each of these media? How would the truth or falsity of the following quotation from *The Selling of the President, 1968* (McGinniss) affect the way you plan your campaign? ". . . a product of the particular chemistry between the voter and the *image* of the candidate. We have to be very clear on this point: that the response is to the *image, not to the man.* . . . It's not what's there that counts, it's what's projected . . . it's not what he projects but rather what the voter receives."

5. Television is called a medium, someone has said, because so little of it is rare, and seldom is it well done. Cite exceptions to this statement.

6. Sydney Harris, the syndicated columnist and critic, explains our nostalgia for old-time radio shows in this way: "Television has failed to grip the audience the way radio did because it leaves little or nothing to the work of the imagination. . . . Whether we are trying to entertain people, or persuade them, we must get them to participate in the imaginative act; else, the more we bombard them with visual bits, the more resistant they become." Do you agree or disagree? Support your position with specific instances.

Glossary

ad lib—Speech or action that has not been written or rehearsed

AFTRA—American Federation of Television and Radio Artists; talent union

ASCAP—American Society of Composers, Authors, and Publishers; collects royalties for performance of copyrighted material

aspect ratio—The proportionate size of the television screen, three units high and four units wide with the long side horizontal

barn doors—Metal covers hinged to the front of a spotlight to regulate the spread of the light beam

blooper—A mistake, usually a slip of the tongue, such as "Open tape, roll talent, cue mike," or the famous one, "I present the President of the United States, Hoobert Heever"

BMI—Broadcast Music Incorporated; collects royalties on copyrighted music performed on radio and television

boom—Microphone suspended on end of a movable metal arm attached to a floor stand

busy—Background so elaborate or detailed that it distracts; design so intricate that it produces a flicker or jiggling effect on television screen

cart—Video or audio tape cartridges cued instantly for commercial messages or music.

CATV—Community antenna television, distributed to receivers via cable from a master antenna

CCTV—Closed circuit television; distributed to specific television receivers but not telecast to the general public

character generator—An electronic process much like a typewriter that inserts lettering into the TV picture.

chroma key—By keying certain colors (usually blue or green) a performer can be inserted in front of slides or film used in newscasts.

clear—To obtain permission to use copyrighted material

coaxial cable—Shielded cable through which television pictures and sound are transmitted

continuity—(1) Script; (2) Content of show; (3) Logically related sequence of events *control room*—Area where director, switcher, technical director, and audio technician work during the program

copy—Any portion of the program that is written word for word

cover shot—Picture which shows entire set or entire group of performers

crawl—Graphics or credits copy mounted on a drum and rotated upward in front of camera

credits—List of people who participated in the production and performance of a television program

cushion—Words or music which can be included or omitted as needed to meet time requirements

cut—An instant switch from one picture to another without fading

definition—The degree or amount of detail clearly visible in a television picture

depth of field—The area in which all objects, located at different distances from camera, appear in focus

dolly—(1) Tripod or pedestal that supports camera and enables it to be moved in all directions; (2) to move camera toward or away from an object

dry run—A rehearsal without cameras

establishing shot—A long shot or a wide shot to orient viewer to the setting or situation

FCC—The Federal Communications Commission, appointed by the President to regulate broadcasting

feed—To transmit or send the television signal from one source to another

film clip—A section clipped from a motion picture to be shown independently of the remainder of the reel

flat—A piece of standing scenery made of a wooden frame covered with muslin or canvas

flip cards—Graphics on cards of same size that can be changed by flipping one after the other on or off the easel or hod

FM—Frequency modulation; static free broadcasting characterized by more faithful reproduction of sound

focal length—Distance from center of lens to surface of camera tube (Short lenses have a wide angle of view; long lenses have a narrow angle of view.)

footcandle—A unit of illumination, the amount of light produced by one candle one foot away from a portion of a sphere or object

graphics—Two-dimensional visuals; cards, flat pictures, printed or lettered signs

hod—An easel for holding graphics or flip cards

image orthicon (I.O.)—Very sensitive camera pickup tube; used in most commercial television studio cameras; refers to either the tube itself or the camera *intercom*—Intercommunication system among studio and control room personnel; headset with or without microphone

key light—Principal source of illumination; sometimes called *modeling light*

kill—to cut out or remove

level—Audio volume; "get a level" means to check the amount of volume

limbo—Any area of the set having no scenic background; used for displays, easels, etc.

live—(1) Direct transmission of a studio program at the time it is originated or performed; (2) turned on; such as a live mike

monitor—A television set used in studio for checking what is being picked up by camera or what is going out on air

multiplexer—An instrument that uses mirrors to reflect pictures from different projectors into one camera

NAB—National Association of Broadcasters, an organization of commercial broadcasters

NAEB—National Association of Educational Broadcasters; an organization of noncommercial or public broadcasters

pan—To move camera horizontally while pedestal remains stationary

pix—An abbreviation for *pictures*

PL—The phone line or intercommunication system among control room staff and studio personnel

pole cats—Extension poles between studio floor and ceiling used to support scenery and graphics

pots—Volume control dials on the audio board

pre-empt—To acquire television time for high priority programs by excluding regularly scheduled programs

props—Properties; objects used for decorating the set or used by performers

Public Broadcasting Service (PBS)—Noncommercial, public broadcasting programs telecast by educational stations

racking—Changing lenses by rotating the lens turret

rear screen projection—A translucent screen onto which a slide or picture is projected from rear and photographed or televised from the front

ride gain—To keep hand on audio control and watch needle which registers amount of volume being fed through audio line

SESAC—The Society of European Stage Authors and Composers; collects royalties on materials it has copyrighted

shot—The picture taken by the television camera

shot sheet—A list in order of the shots a camera is to take

stand by—To stay in position for the program which is about to go on the air

strike—(1) To remove objects no longer needed in the show; (2) to take down scenery after the show

super—The simultaneous showing of two or more full pictures on same screen; often letters or names over a picture

talent—A collective name for all television performers and actors

tally light—The small red light on camera indicating when that camera is on the air; also called *cue light*

Teleprompter—The brand name for a mechanical prompting device with roll of copy mounted in front of camera, visible to the talent

test pattern—The line picture used by technicians to align picture properly

TD—The technical director or switcher, who operates switching controls changing from one camera to another by cutting, dissolving, fading

tilt—To point camera up or down while camera mount remains stationary

truck—To move camera and dolly laterally, left and right

vidicon—A camera picture tube, less sensitive than image orthicon; frequently used in CCTV

visuals—Articles, pictures, signs, properties seen on television (when a distinction is made between two-dimensional and three-dimensional visuals, the two dimensional visuals are called *graphics*)

Zoom—To change focal length of lens in and out, near and far; gives the effect of dollying without moving camera

Index

NTC LANGUAGE ARTS BOOKS

Tandem: Language in Action Series
Point/Counterpoint, *Dufour and Strauss*
Action/Interaction, *Dufour and Strauss*

Writing and Composition
Snap, Crackle & Write, *Schrank*
An Anthology for Young Writers, *Meredith*
Writing in Action, *Meredith*

Reading
Reading by Doing, *Simmons and Palmer*
Literature Alive! *Gamble and Gamble*

Grammar
The Great American Grammar Machine Vol. 1, *Pratt*
The Great American Grammar Machine Vol. 2, *Pratt*

Speech
Person to Person, *Galvin and Book*
Person to Person Workbook, *Galvin and Book*
Speaking by Doing, *Buys, Sills, Beck*
Adventures in the Looking Glass, *Ratliffe and Herman*
Literature Alive! *Gamble and Gamble*
Contemporary Speech, *HopKins and Whitaker*

Journalism
Journalism Today! *Ferguson and Patten*

Media
Understanding Mass Media, *Schrank*
Working with Media, *Hollister*
Media, Messages & Language, *McLuhan, Hutchon, McLuhan*
Understanding the Film, *Johnson and Bone*
Photography in Focus, *Jacobs and Kokrda*
Televising Your Message, *Mitchell and Kirkham*

Theatre
The Dynamics of Acting, *Snyder and Drumsta*
Play Production in the High School, *Beck et al.*
Acting and Directing, *Grandstaff.*
Stagecraft, *Beck*
An Introduction to Theatre and Drama, *Cassady and Cassady*

Mythology
Mythology and You, *Rosenberg and Baker*

Mystery and Science Fiction
The Detective Story, *Schwartz*
You and Science Fiction, *Hollister*

Business Communication
Successful Business Writing, *Sitzmann*
Successful Business Speaking, *Fryar and Thomas*
Successful Interviewing, *Sitzmann and Garcia*
Successful Problem Solving, *Fryar and Thomas*
Working in Groups, *Ratliffe and Stech*